CHARTBOOK
A Reference Grammar

FUNDAMENTALS OF

English
Grammar

FOURTH EDITION

PEARSON
Longman

Betty S. Azar
Stacy A. Hagen

Fundamentals of English Grammar, Fourth Edition Chartbook

Copyright © 2012, 2003, 1992, 1985 by Betty Azar
All rights reserved.

No part of this publication may be reproduced, stored in a retrieval system, or transmitted in any form or by any means, electronic, mechanical, photocopying, recording, or otherwise, without the prior permission of the publisher.

Azar Associates: Shelley Hartle, Editor, and Sue Van Etten, Manager

Pearson Education, 10 Bank Street, White Plains, NY 10606

Staff credits: The people who made up the *Fundamentals of English Grammar, Fourth Edition, Chartbook* team, representing editorial, production, design, and manufacturing, are Dave Dickey, Christine Edmonds, Ann France, and Robert Ruvo.

Text composition: S4Carlisle Publishing Services
Text font: Helvetica
Illustrations: Don Martinetti and Chris Pavely

ISBN 10: 0-13-707141-8
ISBN 13: 978-0-13-707141-8

Printed in the United States of America

1 2 3 4 5 6 7 8 9 10—V057—16 15 14 13 12 11

Contents

Preface to the Fourth Edition viii

Chapter 1   PRESENT TIME 1

1-1   Simple present and present progressive 1
1-2   Forms of the simple present and the present progressive 2
1-3   Frequency adverbs 3
1-4   Singular/plural 4
1-5   Spelling of final *-s/-es* 4
1-6   Non-action verbs 5
1-7   Present verbs: short answers to yes/no questions 6

Chapter 2   PAST TIME 7

2-1   Expressing past time: the simple past 7
2-2   Spelling of *-ing* and *-ed* forms 8
2-3   The principal parts of a verb 9
2-4   Common irregular verbs: a reference list 10
2-5   Regular verbs: pronunciation of *-ed* endings 11
2-6   Simple past and past progressive 12
2-7   Expressing past time: using time clauses 13
2-8   Expressing past habit: *used to* 14

Chapter 3   FUTURE TIME 15

3-1   Expressing future time: *be going to* and *will* 15
3-2   Forms with *be going to* 16
3-3   Forms with *will* 16
3-4   Certainty about the future 17
3-5   *Be going to* vs. *will* 17
3-6   Expressing the future in time clauses and *if*-clauses 18
3-7   Using the present progressive to express future time 18
3-8   Using the simple present to express future time 19
3-9   Immediate future: using *be about to* 19
3-10   Parallel verbs 19

Chapter 4   PRESENT PERFECT AND PAST PERFECT 20

4-1   Past participle 20
4-2   Present perfect with *since* and *for* 21

	4-3	Negative, question, and short-answer forms	22
	4-4	Present perfect with unspecified time	23
	4-5	Simple past vs. present perfect	24
	4-6	Present perfect progressive	25
	4-7	Present perfect progressive vs. present perfect	26
	4-8	Past perfect	27

Chapter 5		**ASKING QUESTIONS**	**28**
	5-1	Yes/no questions and short answers	28
	5-2	Yes/no questions and information questions	29
	5-3	*Where, why, when, what time, how come, what ... for*	30
	5-4	Questions with *who, who(m),* and *what*	30
	5-5	Using *what* + a form of *do*	31
	5-6	Using *which* and *what kind of*	31
	5-7	Using *whose*	32
	5-8	Using *how*	32
	5-9	Using *how often*	33
	5-10	Using *how far*	33
	5-11	Length of time: *it* + *take* and *how long*	34
	5-12	Spoken and written contractions with question words	35
	5-13	More questions with *how*	36
	5-14	Using *how about* and *what about*	36
	5-15	Tag questions	37

Chapter 6		**NOUNS AND PRONOUNS**	**38**
	6-1	Plural forms of nouns	38
	6-2	Pronunciation of final *-s/-es*	39
	6-3	Subjects, verbs, and objects	39
	6-4	Objects of prepositions	40
	6-5	Prepositions of time	40
	6-6	Word order: place and time	41
	6-7	Subject-verb agreement	41
	6-8	Using adjectives to describe nouns	42
	6-9	Using nouns as adjectives	42
	6-10	Personal pronouns: subjects and objects	43
	6-11	Possessive nouns	44
	6-12	Possessive pronouns and adjectives	45
	6-13	Reflexive pronouns	46
	6-14	Singular forms of *other: another* vs. *the other*	47
	6-15	Plural forms of *other: other(s)* vs. *the other(s)*	48
	6-16	Summary of forms of *other*	49

Chapter 7		**MODAL AUXILIARIES**	**50**
	7-1	The form of modal auxiliaries	50
	7-2	Expressing ability: *can* and *could*	51
	7-3	Expressing possibility: *may, might,* and *maybe;* Expressing permission: *may* and *can*	52
	7-4	Using *could* to express possibility	52
	7-5	Polite questions: *may I, could I, can I*	53

	7-6	Polite questions: *would you, could you, will you, can you*	53
	7-7	Expressing advice: *should* and *ought to*	54
	7-8	Expressing advice: *had better*	54
	7-9	Expressing necessity: *have to, have got to, must*	55
	7-10	Expressing lack of necessity: *do not have to;* Expressing prohibition: *must not*	55
	7-11	Making logical conclusions: *must*	55
	7-12	Tag questions with modal auxiliaries	56
	7-13	Giving instructions: imperative sentences	56
	7-14	Making suggestions: *let's* and *why don't*	57
	7-15	Stating preferences: *prefer, like ... better, would rather*	58

Chapter 8 **CONNECTING IDEAS** **59**

	8-1	Connecting ideas with *and*	59
	8-2	Connecting ideas with *but* and *or*	60
	8-3	Connecting ideas with *so*	60
	8-4	Using auxiliary verbs after *but*	60
	8-5	Using *and* + *too, so, either, neither*	61
	8-6	Connecting ideas with *because*	62
	8-7	Connecting ideas with *even though/although*	62

Chapter 9 **COMPARISONS** **63**

	9-1	Making comparisons with *as ... as*	63
	9-2	Comparative and superlative	64
	9-3	Comparative and superlative forms of adjectives and adverbs	65
	9-4	Completing a comparative	66
	9-5	Modifying comparatives	66
	9-6	Comparisons with *less ... than* and *not as ... as*	66
	9-7	Using *more* with nouns	67
	9-8	Repeating a comparative	67
	9-9	Using double comparatives	67
	9-10	Using superlatives	68
	9-11	Using *the same, similar, different, like, alike*	69

Chapter 10 **THE PASSIVE** **70**

	10-1	Active sentences and passive sentences	70
	10-2	Form of the passive	71
	10-3	Transitive and intransitive verbs	72
	10-4	Using the *by*-phrase	73
	10-5	Passive modal auxiliaries	73
	10-6	Using past participles as adjectives (non-progressive passive) ...	74
	10-7	Participial adjectives: *-ed* vs. *-ing*	75
	10-8	*Get* + adjective; *get* + past participle	75
	10-9	Using *be used/accustomed to* and *get used/accustomed to*	76
	10-10	*Used to* vs. *be used to*	76
	10-11	Using *be supposed to*	76

Chapter 11   COUNT/NONCOUNT NOUNS AND ARTICLES **77**

11-1   *A* vs. *an* 77
11-2   Count and noncount nouns 78
11-3   Noncount nouns 79
11-4   More noncount nouns 80
11-5   Using *several, a lot of, many*/*much,* and *a few*/*a little* 80
11-6   Nouns that can be count or noncount 81
11-7   Using units of measure with noncount nouns 81
11-8   Guidelines for article usage 82
11-9   Using *the* or Ø with names 84
11-10 Capitalization 85

Chapter 12   ADJECTIVE CLAUSES **86**

12-1   Adjective clauses: introduction 86
12-2   Using *who* and *that* in adjective clauses to describe people 87
12-3   Using object pronouns in adjective clauses to describe people 88
12-4   Using pronouns in adjective clauses to describe things 89
12-5   Singular and plural verbs in adjective clauses 89
12-6   Using prepositions in adjective clauses 90
12-7   Using *whose* in adjective clauses 90

Chapter 13   GERUNDS AND INFINITIVES **91**

13-1   Verb + gerund 91
13-2   *Go* + *-ing* 91
13-3   Verb + infinitive 92
13-4   Verb + gerund or infinitive 92
13-5   Preposition + gerund 93
13-6   Using *by* and *with* to express how something is done 93
13-7   Using gerunds as subjects; using *it* + infinitive 94
13-8   *It* + infinitive: using *for* (*someone*) 94
13-9   Expressing purpose with *in order to* and *for* 94
13-10 Using infinitives with *too* and *enough* 95

Chapter 14   NOUN CLAUSES **96**

14-1   Noun clauses: introduction 96
14-2   Noun clauses that begin with a question word 97
14-3   Noun clauses that begin with *if* or *whether* 98
14-4   Noun clauses that begin with *that* 98
14-5   Other uses of *that*-clauses 99
14-6   Substituting *so* for a *that*-clause in conversational responses 99
14-7   Quoted speech 100
14-8   Quoted speech vs. reported speech 100
14-9   Verb forms in reported speech 101
14-10 Common reporting verbs: *tell, ask, answer*/*reply* 102

Appendix   SUPPLEMENTARY GRAMMAR CHARTS 103
Unit A: A-1   The present perfect vs. the past perfect 103
           A-2   The past progressive vs. the past perfect 104
           A-3   *Still* vs. *anymore* 104
           A-4   Additional verbs followed by *that*-clauses 105
           A-5   Additional expressions with *be* + *that*-clauses 105
Unit B: B-1   Phrasal verbs . . . .
           B-2   Phrasal verbs: a reference list 107
Unit C: C-1   Preposition combinations: introduction 109
           C-2   Preposition combinations: a reference list 109

Index 111

Preface to the Fourth Edition

Fundamentals of English Grammar Chartbook is a grammar reference for lower intermediate and intermediate English language learners. It contains all the charts found in the student text *Fundamentals of English Grammar, fourth edition.* The information that learners need and want in order to communicate effectively is presented clearly, accurately, and concisely.

The *Chartbook* is a comprehensive reference tool for students and teachers alike. It can be used as a stand-alone text or in conjunction with the *Workbook.* Since the *Workbook* has an answer key, a *Chartbook* plus *Workbook* combination allows learners to study independently. They can investigate and correct their usage problems, expand their usage repertoire by doing self-study practices in the *Workbook,* and find answers to most of their grammar questions in the *Chartbook.*

Teachers and students may find the *Chartbook* plus *Workbook* combination especially useful in writing classes, in tutorials, or in rapid reviews in which grammar is not the main focus but needs attention.

Differences in structure and usage between American English and British English are noted, but the differences are few and relatively insignificant.

A *Teacher's Guide,* which contains background teaching notes for all the charts, as well as step-by-step instructions for in-class use, is also available. Included with the *Teacher's Guide* are ten beyond-the-book *PowerPoint* lessons; they highlight several key grammar structures and provide supplementary reading practice.

Chapter **1**
Present Time

1-1 Simple Present and Present Progressive

Simple Present		
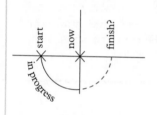	(a) Ann *takes* a shower *every day*.	The SIMPLE PRESENT expresses *daily habits* or *usual activities,* as in (a) and (b).
	(b) I *usually* **read** the newspaper in the morning.	
	(c) Babies **cry**. Birds **fly**.	The simple present expresses *general statements of fact,* as in (c).
	(d) NEGATIVE: It **doesn't snow** in Bangkok.	In general, the simple present is used for events or situations that exist always, usually, or habitually in the past, present, and future.
	(e) QUESTION: **Does** the teacher **speak** slowly?	

Present Progressive		
	(f) Ann can't come to the phone *right now* because she **is taking** a shower.	The PRESENT PROGRESSIVE expresses *an activity that is in progress (is occurring, is happening) right now.*
	(g) I **am reading** my grammar book *right now*.	The event is in progress at the time the speaker is saying the sentence. The event began in the past, is in progress now, and will probably continue into the future.
	(h) Jimmy and Susie are babies. They **are crying**. I can hear them *right now*. Maybe they are hungry.	
	(i) NEGATIVE: It **isn't snowing** *right now*.	FORM: **am, is, are** + **-ing**
	(j) QUESTION: **Is** the teacher **speaking** *right now*?	

1-2 Forms of the Simple Present and the Present Progressive

	Simple Present				Present Progressive			
STATEMENT	I	*work.*			I	*am*	*working.*	
	You	*work.*			You	*are*	*working.*	
	He, She, It	*works.*			He, She, It	*is*	*working.*	
	We	*work.*			We	*are*	*working.*	
	They	*work.*			They	*are*	*working.*	
NEGATIVE	I	*do*	*not*	*work.*	I	*am*	*not*	*working.*
	You	*do*	*not*	*work.*	You	*are*	*not*	*working.*
	He, She, It	*does*	*not*	*work.*	He, She, It	*is*	*not*	*working.*
	We	*do*	*not*	*work.*	We	*are*	*not*	*working.*
	They	*do*	*not*	*work.*	They	*are*	*not*	*working.*
QUESTION	*Do*	I		*work?*	*Am*	I		*working?*
	Do	you		*work?*	*Are*	you		*working?*
	Does	he, she, it		*work?*	*Is*	he, she, it		*working?*
	Do	we		*work?*	*Are*	we		*working?*
	Do	they		*work?*	*Are*	they		*working?*

Contractions

pronoun + *be*	I + am = **I'm** working.
	you, we, they + are = **You're, We're, They're** working.
	he, she, it + is = **He's, She's, It's** working.

do + *not*	does + not = **doesn't** She **doesn't** work.
	do + not = **don't** I **don't** work.

be + *not*	is + not = **isn't** He **isn't** working.
	are + not = **aren't** They **aren't** working.
	(am + not = am not* I am not working.)

*NOTE: *am* and *not* are not contracted.

A dolphin *doesn't walk*. It *swims*.

1-3 Frequency Adverbs

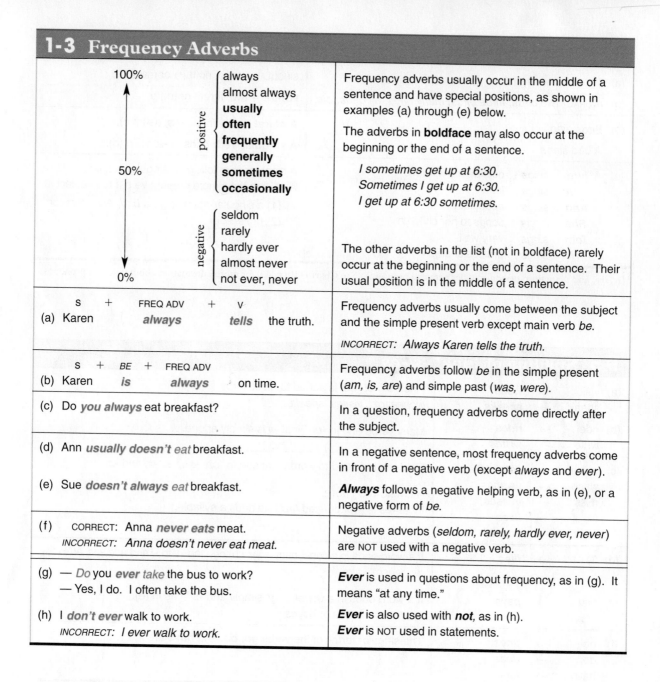

100% — positive — always / almost always / **usually** / **often** / **frequently** / **generally** / **sometimes** / **occasionally** 50% negative — seldom / rarely / hardly ever / almost never / not ever, never 0%	Frequency adverbs usually occur in the middle of a sentence and have special positions, as shown in examples (a) through (e) below. The adverbs in **boldface** may also occur at the beginning or the end of a sentence. *I sometimes get up at 6:30.* *Sometimes I get up at 6:30.* *I get up at 6:30 sometimes.* The other adverbs in the list (not in boldface) rarely occur at the beginning or the end of a sentence. Their usual position is in the middle of a sentence.
S + FREQ ADV + V (a) Karen *always* *tells* the truth.	Frequency adverbs usually come between the subject and the simple present verb except main verb *be*. INCORRECT: *Always Karen tells the truth.*
S + BE + FREQ ADV (b) Karen *is* *always* on time.	Frequency adverbs follow *be* in the simple present (*am, is, are*) and simple past (*was, were*).
(c) Do *you always* eat breakfast?	In a question, frequency adverbs come directly after the subject.
(d) Ann *usually doesn't eat* breakfast. (e) Sue *doesn't always eat* breakfast.	In a negative sentence, most frequency adverbs come in front of a negative verb (except *always* and *ever*). **Always** follows a negative helping verb, as in (e), or a negative form of *be*.
(f) CORRECT: Anna *never eats* meat. INCORRECT: Anna *doesn't never eat meat.*	Negative adverbs (*seldom, rarely, hardly ever, never*) are NOT used with a negative verb.
(g) — Do *you ever take* the bus to work? — Yes, I do. I often take the bus.	**Ever** is used in questions about frequency, as in (g). It means "at any time."
(h) I *don't ever* walk to work. INCORRECT: *I ever walk to work.*	**Ever** is also used with **not**, as in (h). **Ever** is NOT used in statements.

1-4 Singular/Plural

(a) SINGULAR: *one bird*	SINGULAR = one, not two or more
(b) PLURAL: *two birds, three birds, many birds, all birds, etc.*	PLURAL = two, three, or more
(c) Bird*s* sing.	**A plural noun** ends in *-s*, as in (c).
(d) A bird sing*s*.	**A singular verb** ends in *-s*, as in (d).

(e) A *bird* sings outside my window.
     It sings loudly.
     Ann sings beautifully.
     She sings songs to her children.
     Tom sings very well.
     He sings professionally.
	A singular verb follows a singular subject.
	Add *-s* to the simple present verb if the subject is
	(1) a singular noun (e.g., *a bird, Ann, Tom*) or
	(2) *he, she,* or *it.*★

★*He, she,* and *it* are third person singular personal pronouns. See Chart 6-10, p. 43, for more information about personal pronouns.

1-5 Spelling of Final *-s/-es*

(a)	visit →	**visits**	Final *-s*, not *-es*, is added to most verbs.
	speak →	**speaks**	INCORRECT: *visites, speakes*
(b)	ride →	**rides**	Many verbs end in *-e*. Final *-s* is simply added.
	write →	**writes**	
(c)	catch →	**catches**	Final *-es* is added to words that end in *-ch*, *-sh*, *-s*, *-x*, and *-z*.
	wash →	**washes**	
	miss →	**misses**	PRONUNCIATION NOTE:
	fix →	**fixes**	Final *-es* is pronounced /əz/ and adds a syllable.★
	buzz →	**buzzes**	
(d)	fly →	**flies**	If a word ends in a consonant + *-y*, change the *-y* to *-i* and add *-es*, as in (d).
			INCORRECT: *flys*
(e)	pay →	**pays**	If a word ends in a vowel + *-y*, simply add *-s*,★★ as in (e).
			INCORRECT: *paies* or *payes*
(f)	go →	**goes**	The singular forms of the verbs **go**, **do**, and **have** are irregular.
	do →	**does**	
	have →	**has**	

★See Chart 6-1, p. 38, for more information about the pronunciation of final *-s/-es*.

★★Vowels = a, e, i, o, u. Consonants = all other letters in the alphabet.

1-6 Non-Action Verbs

(a) I **know** Ms. Chen.
    INCORRECT: I am knowing Ms. Chen.
 	
(b) I'm hungry. I **want** a sandwich.
    INCORRECT: I am wanting a sandwich.
 	
(c) This book **belongs** to Mikhail.
    INORRECT: This book is belonging to Mikhail.
	Some verbs are generally not used in progressive tenses. These verbs are called "non-action verbs."* They express a situation that exists, not an action in progress.

Non-action Verbs

hear	believe	be	own	need	like	forget
see	think	exist	have	want	love	remember
sound	understand		possess	prefer	hate	
	know	seem	belong			agree
	mean	look like				disagree

COMPARE: (d) I **think** that grammar is easy. (e) I **am thinking** about grammar right now. (f) Tom **has** a car. (g) I**'m having** a good time.	**Think** and **have** can be used in the progressive. In (d): When **think** means "believe," it is non-progressive. In (e): When **think** expresses thoughts that are going through a person's mind, it can be progressive. In (f): When **have** means "own" or expresses possession, it is not used in the progressive. In (g): In expressions where **have** does not mean "own" (e.g., *have a good time, have a bad time, have trouble, have a problem, have lunch, have a snack, have company, have an operation*), **have** can be used in the progressive.

*Non-action verbs are also called "non-progressive" or "stative" verbs.

Bruno *is* an excellent cook.

1-7 Present Verbs: Short Answers to Yes/No Questions

	Question	Short Answer	Long Answer
QUESTIONS WITH *DO/DOES*	*Does* Bob *like* tea?	Yes, he *does*. No, he *doesn't*.	Yes, he likes tea. No, he doesn't like tea.
	Do you *like* tea?	Yes, I *do*. No, I *don't*.	Yes, I like tea. No, I don't like tea.
QUESTIONS WITH *BE*	*Are* you *studying*?	Yes, I *am*.* No, I *'m not*.	Yes, I am (I'm) studying. No, I'm not studying.
	Is Yoko a student?	Yes, she *is*.* No, she *'s not*. OR No, she *isn't*.	Yes, she is (she's) a student. No, she's not a student. OR No, she isn't a student.
	Are they *studying*?	Yes, they *are*.* No, they *'re not*. OR No, they *aren't*.	Yes, they are (they're) studying. No, they're not studying. OR No, they aren't studying.

Am, is, and *are* are NOT contracted with pronouns in short answers.

INCORRECT SHORT ANSWERS: *Yes, I'm. Yes, she's. Yes, they're.*

Q: *Are* the children *building* a sandcastle?
A: Yes, they *are*.

Chapter 2
Past Time

2-1 Expressing Past Time: The Simple Past

(a) Mary *walked* downtown *yesterday*. (b) I *slept* for eight hours *last night*.	The simple past is used to talk about activities or situations that began and ended in the past (e.g., *yesterday, last night, two days ago, in 2010*).
(c) Bob *stayed* home yesterday morning. (d) Our plane *landed* on time last night.	Most simple past verbs are formed by adding *-ed* to a verb, as in (a), (c), and (d).
(e) I *ate* breakfast this morning. (f) Sue *took* a taxi to the airport yesterday.	Some verbs have irregular past forms, as in (b), (e), and (f). See Chart 2-4.
(g) I *was* busy yesterday. (h) They *were* at home last night.	The simple past forms of *be* are *was* and *were*.

Forms of the Simple Past: Regular Verbs

STATEMENT	I, You, She, He, It, We, They *worked* yesterday.
NEGATIVE	I, You, She, He, It, We, They *did not* (*didn't*) *work* yesterday.
QUESTION	*Did* I, you, she, he, it, we, they *work* yesterday?
SHORT ANSWER	Yes, I, you, she, he, it, we, they *did*. OR No, I, you, she, he, it, we, they *didn't*.

Forms of the Simple Past: *Be*

STATEMENT	I, She, He, It *was* in class yesterday. We, You, They *were* in class yesterday.
NEGATIVE	I, She, He, It *was not* (*wasn't*) in class yesterday. We, You, They *were not* (*weren't*) in class yesterday.
QUESTION	*Was* I, she, he, it in class yesterday? *Were* we, you, they in class yesterday?
SHORT ANSWER	Yes, I, she, he, it *was*. Yes, we, you, they *were*. No, I, she, he, it *wasn't*. No, we, you, they *weren't*.

2-2 Spelling of -ing and -ed Forms

End of Verb	Double the Consonant?	Simple Form	-ing	-ed	
-e	NO	(a) smile hope	smiling hoping	smiled hoped	**-ing** form: Drop the **-e**, add **-ing**. **-ed** form: Just add **-d**.
Two Consonants	NO	(b) help learn	helping learning	helped learned	If the verb ends in two consonants, just add **-ing** or **-ed**.
Two Vowels + One Consonant	NO	(c) rain heat	raining heating	rained heated	If the verb ends in two vowels + a consonant, just add **-ing** or **-ed**.
One Vowel + One Consonant	YES	ONE-SYLLABLE VERBS			If the verb has one syllable and ends in one vowel + one consonant, double the consonant to make the **-ing** or **-ed** form.*
		(d) stop plan	stopping planning	stopped planned	
	NO	TWO-SYLLABLE VERBS			If the first syllable of a two-syllable verb is stressed, do not double the consonant.
		(e) vísit óffer	visiting offering	visited offered	
	YES	(f) prefér admít	preferring admitting	preferred admitted	If the second syllable of a two-syllable verb is stressed, double the consonant.
-y	NO	(g) play enjoy	playing enjoying	played enjoyed	If the verb ends in a vowel + **-y**, keep the **-y**. Do not change the **-y** to **-i**.
		(h) worry study	worrying studying	worried studied	If the verb ends in a consonant + **-y**, keep the **-y** for the **-ing** form, but change the **-y** to **-i** to make the **-ed** form.
-ie		(i) die tie	dying tying	died tied	**-ing** form: Change the **-ie** to **-y** and add **-ing**. **-ed** form: Just add **-d**.

*EXCEPTIONS: Do not double "w" or "x": *snow, snowing, snowed, fix, fixing, fixed.*

2-3 The Principal Parts of a Verb

Regular Verbs

SIMPLE FORM	SIMPLE PAST	PAST PARTICIPLE	PRESENT PARTICIPLE
finish	finished	finished	finishing
stop	stopped	stopped	stopping
hope	hoped	hoped	hoping
wait	waited	waited	waiting
play	played	played	playing
try	tried	tried	trying

Irregular Verbs

see	saw	seen	seeing
make	made	made	making
sing	sang	sung	singing
eat	ate	eaten	eating
put	put	put	putting
go	went	gone	going

Principal Parts of a Verb

(1) THE SIMPLE FORM	English verbs have four principal forms, or "parts." **The simple form** is the form that is found in a dictionary. It is the base form with no endings on it (no final **-s**, **-ed**, or **-ing**).
(2) THE SIMPLE PAST	**The simple past** ends in **-ed** for regular verbs. Most verbs are regular, but many common verbs have irregular past forms. See the reference list of irregular verbs that follows in Chart 2-4.
(3) THE PAST PARTICIPLE	**The past participle** also ends in **-ed** for regular verbs. Some verbs are irregular. It is used in perfect tenses (Chapter 4) and the passive (Chapter 10).
(4) THE PRESENT PARTICIPLE	**The present participle** ends in **-ing** (for both regular and irregular verbs). It is used in progressive tenses (e.g., the present progressive and the past progressive).

2-4 Common Irregular Verbs: A Reference List

SIMPLE FORM	SIMPLE PAST	PAST PARTICIPLE	SIMPLE FORM	SIMPLE PAST	PAST PARTICIPLE
be	was, were	been	lend	lent	lent
beat	beat	beaten	let	let	let
become	became	become	lie	lay	lain
begin	began	begun	light	lit/lighted	lit/lighted
bend	bent	bent	lose	lost	lost
bite	bit	bitten	make	made	made
blow	blew	blown	mean	meant	meant
break	broke	broken	meet	met	met
bring	brought	brought	pay	paid	paid
build	built	built	put	put	put
burn	burned/burnt	burned/burnt	quit	quit	quit
buy	bought	bought	read	read	read
catch	caught	caught	ride	rode	ridden
choose	chose	chosen	ring	rang	rung
come	came	come	rise	rose	risen
cost	cost	cost	run	ran	run
cut	cut	cut	say	said	said
dig	dug	dug	see	saw	seen
do	did	done	sell	sold	sold
draw	drew	drawn	send	sent	sent
dream	dreamed/dreamt	dreamed/dreamt	set	set	set
drink	drank	drunk	shake	shook	shaken
drive	drove	driven	shoot	shot	shot
eat	ate	eaten	shut	shut	shut
fall	fell	fallen	sing	sang	sung
feed	fed	fed	sink	sank	sunk
feel	felt	felt	sit	sat	sat
fight	fought	fought	sleep	slept	slept
find	found	found	slide	slid	slid
fit	fit	fit	speak	spoke	spoken
fly	flew	flown	spend	spent	spent
forget	forgot	forgotten	spread	spread	spread
forgive	forgave	forgiven	stand	stood	stood
freeze	froze	frozen	steal	stole	stolen
get	got	got/gotten	stick	stuck	stuck
give	gave	given	swim	swam	swum
go	went	gone	take	took	taken
grow	grew	grown	teach	taught	taught
hang	hung	hung	tear	tore	torn
have	had	had	tell	told	told
hear	heard	heard	think	thought	thought
hide	hid	hidden	throw	threw	thrown
hit	hit	hit	understand	understood	understood
hold	held	held	upset	upset	upset
hurt	hurt	hurt	wake	woke/waked	woken/waked
keep	kept	kept	wear	wore	worn
know	knew	known	win	won	won
leave	left	left	write	wrote	written

2-5 Regular Verbs: Pronunciation of -ed Endings

(a)	talked	=	talk/t/	Final **-ed** is pronounced /t/ after voiceless sounds.
	stopped	=	stop/t/	You make a voiceless sound by pushing air through your mouth.
	hissed	=	hiss/t/	No sound comes from your throat.
	watched	=	watch/t/	Examples of voiceless sounds: /k/, /p/, /s/, /ch/, /sh/.
	washed	=	wash/t/	
(b)	called	=	call/d/	Final **-ed** is pronounced /d/ after voiced sounds.
	rained	=	rain/d/	You make a voiced sound from your throat. Your voice box vibrates.
	lived	=	live/d/	Examples of voiced sounds: /l/, /n/, /v/, /b/, and all vowel sounds.
	robbed	=	rob/d/	
	stayed	=	stay/d/	
(c)	waited	=	wait/əd/	Final **-ed** is pronounced /əd/ after "t" and "d" sounds.
	needed	=	need/əd/	Adding /əd/ adds a syllable to a word.

The movie star *waved* at me.

2-6 Simple Past and Past Progressive

Simple Past	(a) Mary *walked* downtown yesterday. (b) I *slept* for eight hours last night.	The SIMPLE PAST is used to talk about *an activity or situation that began and ended at a particular time in the past* (e.g., *yesterday, last night, two days ago, in 2007*), as in (a) and (b).
Past Progressive	(c) I sat down at the dinner table at 6:00 P.M. yesterday. Tom came to my house at 6:10 P.M. I *was eating* dinner *when Tom came.* (d) I went to bed at 10:00. The phone rang at 11:00. I *was sleeping* when the phone rang.	The PAST PROGRESSIVE expresses *an activity that was in progress (was occurring, was happening)* at a point of time in the past (e.g., *at 6:10*) or at the time of another action (e.g., *when Tom came*). In (c): eating was in progress at 6:10; eating was in progress *when Tom came.* FORM: **was/were + -ing**

(e) **When** the phone rang, I was sleeping. (f) The phone rang **while** I was sleeping.	**when** = at that time **while** = during that time Examples (e) and (f) have the same meaning.

Forms of the Past Progressive

STATEMENT		I, She, He, It *was working.* You, We, They *were working.*	
NEGATIVE		I, She, He, It *was not* (*wasn't*) *working.* You, We, They *were not* (*weren't*) *working.*	
QUESTION	*Was* *Were*	I, she, he, it *working?* you, we, they *working?*	
SHORT ANSWER	Yes, No,	I, she, he, it *was.* I, she, he, it *wasn't.*	Yes, you, we, they *were.* No, you, we, they *weren't.*

2-7 Expressing Past Time: Using Time Clauses

time clause   main clause
(a) *After I finished my work,* *I went to bed.*
 	
    main clause   time clause
(b) *I went to bed* *after I finished my work.*
	After I finished my work = a time clause*
	I went to bed = a main clause
	
	Examples (a) and (b) have the same meaning.
	
	A time clause can
	    (1) come in front of a main clause, as in (a).
	    (2) follow a main clause, as in (b).

(c) I went to bed *after* I finished my work. (d) *Before* I went to bed, I finished my work. (e) I stayed up *until* I finished my work. (f) *As soon as* I finished my work, I went to bed. (g) The phone rang *while* I was watching TV. (h) *When* the phone rang, I was watching TV.	These words introduce time clauses: **after** **before** **until** } + *subject and verb* = a time clause **as soon as** **while** **when**
	In (e): *until* = to that time and then no longer** In (f): *as soon as* = immediately after

	PUNCTUATION: Put a comma at the end of a time clause when the time clause comes first in a sentence (comes in front of the main clause):
	    time clause + comma + main clause
	    *main clause + **no** comma + time clause*

(i) When the phone *rang,* I *answered* it.	In a sentence with a time clause introduced by *when*, both the time clause verb and the main verb can be simple past. In this case, the action in the *when*-clause happened first. In (i): First: *The phone rang.* Then: *I answered it.*
(j) While I *was doing* my homework, my roommate *was watching* TV.	In (j): When two actions are in progress at the same time, the past progressive can be used in both parts of the sentence.

*A *clause* is a structure that has a subject and a verb.

****Until** can also be used to say that something does NOT happen before a particular time: *I **didn't** go to bed **until** I finished my work.*

2-8 Expressing Past Habit: *Used To*

(a) I *used to live* with my parents. Now I live in my own apartment.	***Used to*** expresses a past situation or habit that no longer exists at present.
(b) Ann *used to be* afraid of dogs, but now she likes dogs.	FORM: ***used to*** + *the simple form of a verb*
(c) Al *used to smoke,* but he doesn't anymore.	
(d) *Did* you *used to live* in Paris? (OR *Did* you *use to live* in Paris?)	QUESTION FORM: ***did*** + *subject* + ***used to*** (OR ***did*** + *subject* + ***use to***)★
(e) I *didn't used to drink* coffee at breakfast, but now I always have coffee in the morning. (OR I *didn't use to drink* coffee.)	NEGATIVE FORM: ***didn't used to*** (OR ***didn't use to***)★ *Didn't use(d) to* occurs infrequently. More commonly, people use *never* to express a negative idea with *used to,* as in (f).
(f) I *never used to drink* coffee at breakfast, but now I always have coffee in the morning.	

★Both forms (***used to*** and ***use to***) are possible in questions and negatives. English language authorities do not agree on which is preferable. This book uses both forms.

The volcano *used to be* quiet. Now it's active.

Chapter 3
Future Time

3-1 Expressing Future Time: *Be Going To* and *Will*

Future		
 ─────────┼─────×── │	(a) I *am going to leave* at nine tomorrow morning. (b) I *will leave* at nine tomorrow morning.	*Be going to* and *will* are used to express future time. Examples (a) and (b) have the same meaning. Sometimes *will* and *be going to* express different meanings. The differences are discussed in Chart 3-5.
(c) Sam *is* in his office *this morning*. (d) Ann *was* in her office *this morning* at eight, but now she's at a meeting. (e) Bob *is going to be* in his office *this morning* after his dentist appointment.		*Today*, *tonight*, and *this* + *morning*, *afternoon*, *evening*, *week*, *etc.*, can express present, past, or future time, as in (c) through (e).

NOTE: The use of *shall* (with *I* or *we*) to express future time is possible but is infrequent and quite formal; for example: *I shall* leave at nine tomorrow morning. *We shall* leave at ten tomorrow morning.

The dog *is going to go to sleep* soon.

3-2 Forms with *Be Going To*

(a) We *are going to* **be** late. (b) She*'s going to* **come** tomorrow. INCORRECT: *She's going to comes tomorrow.*	***Be going to*** is followed by the simple form of the verb, as in (a) and (b).

(c) *Am*   I
  Is   he, she, it } *going to be* late?
  Are   they, we, you
	QUESTION FORM: ***be*** + *subject* + ***going to***

(d)   I   *am not*
  He, She, It   *is not* } *going to be* late.
  They, We, You   *are not*
	NEGATIVE FORM: ***be*** + ***not*** + ***going to***

(e) "Hurry up! We're *gonna* be late!"	***Be going to*** is more common in speaking and informal writing than in formal writing. In informal speaking, it is sometimes pronounced "gonna" /gənə/. "Gonna" is not usually a written form.

3-3 Forms with *Will*

STATEMENT	I, You, She, He, It, We, They *will come* tomorrow.
NEGATIVE	I, You, She, He, It, We, They *will not* (*won't*) *come* tomorrow.
QUESTION	*Will* I, you, she, he, it, we, they *come* tomorrow?
SHORT ANSWER	Yes, No, } I, you, she, he, it, we, they { *will.** *won't.*
CONTRACTIONS	I*'ll* she*'ll* we*'ll* you*'ll* he*'ll* they*'ll* it*'ll*	***Will*** is usually contracted with pronouns in both speech and informal writing.
	Bob + *will* = "Bob*'ll*" the teacher + *will* = "the teacher*'ll*"	***Will*** is often contracted with nouns in speech, but usually not in writing.

*Pronouns are NOT contracted with helping verbs in short answers.
  CORRECT: *Yes, I will.*
  INCORRECT: *Yes, I'll.*

3-4 Certainty About the Future

100% sure	(a) I *will be* in class tomorrow. OR I *am going to be* in class tomorrow.	In (a): The speaker uses **will** or **be going to** because he feels sure about his future activity. He is stating a fact about the future.

90% sure	(b) Po *will probably be* in class tomorrow.
	OR
	Po *is probably going to be* in class tomorrow.
	
	(c) Anna *probably won't be* in class tomorrow.
	OR
	Anna *probably isn't going to be* in class tomorrow.
		In (b): The speaker uses **probably** to say that he expects Po to be in class tomorrow, but he is not 100% sure. He's almost sure, but not completely sure.
		
		Word order with **probably:***
		(1) in a statement, as in (b):
		   helping verb + **probably**
		(2) with a negative verb, as in (c):
		   probably + *helping verb*

50% sure	(d) Ali *may come* to class tomorrow. OR Ali *may not come* to class tomorrow. I don't know what he's going to do.	**May** expresses a future possibility: maybe something will happen, and maybe it won't happen.** In (d): The speaker is saying that maybe Ali will come to class, or maybe he won't come to class. The speaker is guessing.
	(e) *Maybe* Ali *will come* to class, and *maybe* he *won't*. OR *Maybe* Ali *is going to come* to class, and *maybe* he *isn't*.	**Maybe** + **will/be going to** gives the same meaning as **may**. Examples (d) and (e) have the same meaning. **Maybe** comes at the beginning of a sentence.

*__Probably__ is a midsentence adverb. See Chart 1-3, p. 3, for more information about the placement of midsentence adverbs.
**See Chart 7-3, p. 52, for more information about *may*.

3-5 *Be Going To* vs. *Will*

(a) She *is going to succeed* because she works hard. (b) She *will succeed* because she works hard.	**Be going to** and **will** mean the same when they are used to make predictions about the future. Examples (a) and (b) have the same meaning.
(c) I bought some wood because I *am going to build* a bookcase for my apartment.	**Be going to** (but not **will**) is used to express a prior plan (i.e., a plan made before the moment of speaking). In (c): The speaker plans to build a bookcase.
(d) This chair is too heavy for you to carry alone. I *'ll help* you.	**Will** (but not **be going to**) is used to express a decision the speaker makes at the moment of speaking. In (d): The speaker decides or volunteers to help at the immediate present moment; he did not have a prior plan or intention to help.

3-6 Expressing the Future in Time Clauses and *If*-Clauses

(a) *Before I go* to class tomorrow, I'm going to eat breakfast. *time clause*	In (a) and (b): *before I go to class tomorrow* is a future time clause. **before** **after** **when** } + *subject and verb* = a time clause **as soon as** **until** **while**
(b) I'm going to eat breakfast *before I go to class tomorrow.* *time clause*	
(c) *Before I go* home tonight, I'm going to stop at the market. (d) I'm going to eat dinner at 6:00 tonight. *After I eat dinner,* I'm going to study in my room. (e) I'll give Rita your message *when I see* her. (f) It's raining right now. *As soon as the rain* **stops,** I'm going to walk downtown. (g) I'll stay home *until the rain* **stops.** (h) *While you're at school tomorrow,* I'll be at work.	The simple present is used in a future time clause. **Will** and **be going to** are NOT used in a future time clause. INCORRECT: Before I will go to class, I'm going to eat breakfast. INCORRECT: Before I am going to go to class tomorrow, I'm going to eat breakfast. All of the example sentences (c) through (h) contain future time clauses.
(i) Maybe it will rain tomorrow. *If it* **rains** *tomorrow,* I'm going to stay home.	In (i): *If it rains tomorrow* is an *if*-clause. *if* + *subject and verb* = an *if*-clause When the meaning is future, the simple present (not **will** or **be going to**) is used in an *if*-clause.

3-7 Using the Present Progressive to Express Future Time

(a) Tim *is going to come* to the party tomorrow. (b) Tim *is coming* to the party tomorrow. (c) We*'re going to go* to a movie tonight. (d) We*'re going* to a movie tonight. (e) I*'m going to stay* home this evening. (f) I*'m staying* home this evening. (g) Ann *is going to fly* to Chicago next week. (h) Ann *is flying* to Chicago next week.	The present progressive can be used to express future time. Each pair of example sentences has the same meaning. The present progressive describes *definite plans for the future, plans that were made before the moment of speaking.* A future meaning for the present progressive is indicated either by future time words (e.g., *tomorrow*) or by the situation.*
(i) You*'re going to laugh* when you hear this joke. (j) INCORRECT: *You're laughing when you hear this joke.*	The present progressive is NOT used for predictions about the future. In (i): The speaker is predicting a future event. In (j): The present progressive is not possible; laughing is a prediction, not a planned future event.

*COMPARE: Present situation: *Look! Mary's coming. Do you see her?*
            Future situation: *Are you planning to come to the party? Mary's coming. So is Alex.*

3-8 Using the Simple Present to Express Future Time

(a) My plane *arrives* at 7:35 *tomorrow evening*. (b) Tim's new job *starts* next week. (c) The semester *ends* in two more weeks. (d) There *is* a meeting at ten *tomorrow morning*.	The simple present can express future time when events are on a definite schedule or timetable. Only a few verbs are used in the simple present to express future time. The most common are *arrive*, *leave*, *start*, *begin*, *end*, *finish*, *open*, *close*, *be*.
(e) INCORRECT: *I wear my new suit to the wedding next week.* CORRECT: *I am wearing/am going to wear* my new suit to the wedding next week.	Most verbs CANNOT be used in the simple present to express future time. For example, in (e): The verb *wear* does not express an event on a schedule or timetable. It cannot be used in the simple present to express future time.

3-9 Immediate Future: Using *Be About To*

(a) Ann's bags are packed, and she is wearing her coat. She *is about to leave* for the airport. (b) Shhh. The movie *is about to begin*.	The idiom *be about to do something* expresses an activity that will happen *in the immediate future*, usually within minutes or seconds. In (a): Ann is going to leave sometime in the next few minutes. In (b): The movie is going to start in the next few minutes.

3-10 Parallel Verbs

V *and* V (a) Jim *makes* his bed *and* *cleans* up his room every morning. (b) Anita *called* and *told* me about her new job.	Often a subject has two verbs that are connected by *and*. We say that the two verbs are parallel: V + *and* + V *makes and cleans* = parallel verbs
(c) Ann *is cooking* dinner and (*is*) *talking* on the phone at the same time. (d) I *will stay* home and (*will*) *study* tonight. (e) I *am going to stay* home and (*am going to*) *study* tonight.	It is not necessary to repeat a helping verb (an auxiliary verb) when two verbs are the same tense and are connected by *and*.

Chapter 4

Present Perfect and Past Perfect

4-1 Past Participle

	Simple Form	Simple Past	Past Participle
REGULAR VERBS	finish stop wait	finished stopped waited	finished stopped waited
IRREGULAR VERBS	see make put	saw made put	seen made put

The **past participle** is one of the principal parts of a verb. (See Chart 2-3, p. 9.)

The past participle is used in the PRESENT PERFECT tense and the PAST PERFECT tense.*

The past participle of regular verbs is the same as the simple past form: both end in *-ed*.

See Chart 2-4, p. 10, or the inside front and back covers for a list of irregular verbs.

*The past participle is also used in the passive. See Chapter 10.

see — saw — seen

4-2 Present Perfect with *Since* and *For*

	(a) I**'ve been** in class *since ten o'clock this morning.* (b) We **have known** Ben *for ten years.* We met him ten years ago. We still know him today. We are friends.	The present perfect tense is used in sentences with **since** and **for** to express situations that began in the past and continue to the present. In (a): Class started at ten. I am still in class now, at the moment of speaking. INCORRECT: *I am in class since ten o'clock this morning.*

(c)	I *have* You *have* She, He, It *has* } *been* here for one hour. We *have* They *have*	FORM: **have/has** + *past participle* CONTRACTED FORMS: *I've, You've, He's, She's, It's, We've, They've.*

Since

(d) I *have been* here {	*since* eight o'clock. *since* Tuesday. *since* 2009 *since* yesterday. *since* last month.	**Since** is followed by the mention of a *specific point in time:* an hour, a day, a month, a year, etc. **Since** expresses the idea that something began at a specific time in the past and continues to the present.

(e) CORRECT: I *have lived* here since May.* CORRECT: I *have been* here since May. (f) INCORRECT: *I am living here since May.* (g) INCORRECT: *I live here since May.* (h) INCORRECT: *I lived here since May.* (i) INCORRECT: *I was here since May.*	Notice the incorrect sentences: In (f): The present progressive is NOT used. In (g): The simple present is NOT used. In (h) and (i): The simple past is NOT used.

	MAIN CLAUSE (present perfect)	SINCE-CLAUSE (simple past)
(j)	I *have lived* here	*since* I *was* a child.
(k)	Al *has met* many people	*since* he *came* here.

> **Since** may also introduce a time clause (i.e., a subject and verb may follow **since**).

 Notice in the examples: The present perfect is used in the main clause; the simple past is used in the *since*-clause.

For

(l) I *have been* here {	*for* ten minutes. *for* two hours. *for* five days. *for* about three weeks. *for* almost six months. *for* many years. *for* a long time.	**For** is followed by the mention of a *length of time:* two minutes, three hours, four days, five weeks, etc.). NOTE: If the noun ends in **-s** (*hours, days, weeks, etc.*), use **for** in the time expression, not **since**.

*Also correct: *I **have been living** here since May.* See Chart 4-6 for a discussion of the present perfect progressive.

4-3 Negative, Question, and Short-Answer Forms

Negative

(a) I *have not* (*haven't*) *seen* Tom since lunch.	NEGATIVE: **have/has** + **not** + past participle
(b) Ann *has not* (*hasn't*) *eaten* for several hours.	NEGATIVE CONTRACTIONS: **have** + **not** = **haven't** **has** + **not** = **hasn't**

Question

(c) *Have you seen Tom?*	QUESTION: **have/has** + subject + past participle
(d) *Has Ann eaten?*	
(e) How long *have you lived* here?	
(f) — Have you *ever* met a famous person? — No, I've *never* met a famous person.	In (f): **ever** = in your lifetime; from the time you were born to the present moment. Questions with **ever** frequently use the present perfect. When answering questions with **ever**, speakers often use **never**. **Never** is frequently used with the present perfect. In the answer to (f), the speaker is saying: "No, I haven't met a famous person from the time I was born to the present moment."

Short Answer

(g) — Have you seen Tom? — *Yes, I* **have**. OR *No, I* **haven't**.	SHORT ANSWER: **have/haven't** or **has/hasn't** NOTE: The helping verb in the short answer is not contracted with the pronoun. INCORRECT: *Yes, I've.* OR *Yes, he's.*
(h) — Has Ann eaten lunch? — *Yes, she* **has**. OR *No, she* **hasn't**.	

Q: *Has* the bird *caught* the worm?
A: *No, it* **hasn't**.

Toshi has already eaten lunch.

Eva hasn't eaten lunch yet.

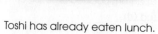

now — *before now* — *time?* ✗ ✗	(a) Toshi *has **just** eaten* lunch. (b) Jim *has **recently** changed* jobs.	The PRESENT PERFECT expresses an activity or situation that occurred (or did not occur) *before now, at some unspecified or unknown time in the past.* Common time words that express this idea are *just, recently, already, yet, ever, never.* In (a): Toshi's lunch occurred before the present time. The *exact* time is not mentioned; it is unimportant or unknown.
now — *before now* ✗✗✗ ✗	(c) Pete *has eaten* at that restaurant ***many times***. (d) I *have eaten* there ***twice***.	An activity may be repeated two, several, or more times *before now,* at *unspecified times in the past,* as in (c) and (d).
	(e) Pete *has **already** left*. OR Pete *has left **already***.	In (e): ***Already*** is used in affirmative statements. It can come after the helping verb or at the end of the sentence. Idea of ***already:*** Something happened before now, before this time.
	(f) Min *hasn't left **yet***.	In (f): ***Yet*** is used in negative statements and comes at the end of the sentence. Idea of ***yet:*** Something did not happen before now (up to this time), but it may happen in the future.
	(g) *Have* you ***already*** *left*? *Have* you *left **already***? *Have* you *left **yet***?	In (g): Both ***yet*** and ***already*** can be used in questions.

4-5 Simple Past vs. Present Perfect

SIMPLE PAST (a) I **finished** my work *two hours ago*. PRESENT PERFECT (b) I **have** already **finished** my work.	In (a): I finished my work at a specific time in the past (*two hours ago*). In (b): I finished my work at an unspecified time in the past (*sometime before now*).
SIMPLE PAST (c) I **was** in Europe *last year / three years ago / in 2006 / in 2008 and 2010 / when I was ten years old*. PRESENT PERFECT (d) I **have been** in Europe *many times / several times / a couple of times / once / (no mention of time)*.	The SIMPLE PAST expresses an activity that occurred at a specific time (or times) in the past, as in (a) and (c). The PRESENT PERFECT expresses an activity that occurred at an unspecified time (or times) in the past, as in (b) and (d).
SIMPLE PAST (e) Ann **was** in Miami *for two weeks*. PRESENT PERFECT (f) Bob **has been in** Miami for *two weeks / since May 1st*.	In (e): In sentences where **for** is used in a time expression, the simple past expresses an activity that began and ended in the past. In (f): In sentences with **for** or **since,** the present perfect expresses an activity that began in the past and continues to the present.

Ann *has been* late for dinner *twice this week.*

4-6 Present Perfect Progressive

Al and Ann are in their car right now. They are driving home. It is now four o'clock. (a) They ***have been driving*** since two o'clock. (b) They ***have been driving*** for two hours. They will be home soon.	The PRESENT PERFECT PROGRESSIVE talks about *how long* an activity has been in progress before now. NOTE: Time expressions with ***since***, as in (a), and ***for***, as in (b), are frequently used with this tense. STATEMENT: ***have/has*** + ***been*** + ***-ing***
(c) How long ***have they been driving***?	QUESTION: ***have/has*** + *subject* + ***been*** + ***-ing***

Present Progressive vs. Present Perfect Progressive

Present Progressive	(d) Po *is sitting* in class right now.	The PRESENT PROGRESSIVE describes an activity that is in progress right now, as in (d). It does not discuss duration (length of time). INCORRECT: *Po has been sitting in class right now.*
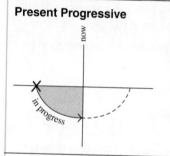		
Present Perfect Progressive	Po is sitting at his desk in class. He sat down at nine o'clock. It is now nine-thirty. (e) Po *has been sitting* in class since nine o'clock. (f) Po *has been sitting* in class for thirty minutes.	The PRESENT PERFECT PROGRESSIVE expresses the **duration** (length of time) of an activity that began in the past and is in progress right now. INCORRECT: *Po is sitting in class since nine o'clock.*
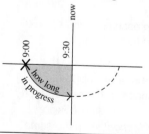		

(g) CORRECT: I *know* Yoko. (h) INCORRECT: *I am knowing Yoko.* (i) CORRECT: I *have known* Yoko *for* two years. (j) INCORRECT: *I have been knowing Yoko for two years.*	NOTE: Non-action verbs (e.g., *know, like, own, belong*) are generally not used in the progressive tenses.* In (i): With non-action verbs, the present perfect is used with ***since*** or ***for*** to express the duration of a situation that began in the past and continues to the present.

*See Chart 1-6, Non-Action Verbs, p. 5.

4-7 Present Perfect Progressive vs. Present Perfect

Present Perfect Progressive

(a) Gina and Tarik are talking on the phone. They *have been talking* on the phone for 20 minutes.	The PRESENT PERFECT PROGRESSIVE expresses the **duration of present *activities*,** using action verbs, as in (a). The activity began in the past and is still in progress.

Present Perfect

(b) Gina *has talked* to Tarik on the phone many times (before now).
(c) *INCORRECT: Gina has been talking to Tarik on the phone many times.*
 	
(d) Gina *has known* Tarik for two years.
(e) *INCORRECT: Gina has been knowing Tarik for two years.*
	The PRESENT PERFECT expresses
	  (1) repeated activities that occur at **unspecified times in the past,** as in (b), OR
	  (2) the **duration of present *situations*,** as in (d), using non-action verbs.

Present Perfect Progressive and Present Perfect

(f) I *have been living* here for six months. OR (g) I *have lived* here for six months. (h) Ed *has been wearing* glasses since he was ten. OR Ed *has worn* glasses since he was ten. (i) I*'ve been going* to school ever since I was five years old. OR I*'ve gone* to school ever since I was five years old.	For some (not all) verbs, duration can be expressed by either the present perfect or the present perfect progressive. Examples (f) and (g) have essentially the same meaning, and both are correct. Often either tense can be used with verbs that express the **duration of usual or habitual activities/situations** (things that happen daily or regularly), e.g., *live, work, teach, smoke, wear glasses, play chess, go to school, read the same newspaper every morning, etc.*

4-8 Past Perfect

Situation:

Jack left his apartment at 2:00. Sue arrived at his apartment at 2:15 and knocked on the door.

(a) When Sue arrived, Jack wasn't there. He **had left**.

The PAST PERFECT is used when the speaker is talking about two different events at two different times in the past; one event ends before the second event happens.

In (a): There are two events, and both happened in the past: *Jack left his apartment. Sue arrived at his apartment.*

To show the time relationship between the two events, we use the past perfect (**had left**) to say that the first event (Jack leaving his apartment) was completed before the second event (Sue arriving at his apartment) occurred.

(b) Jack **had left** his apartment when Sue arrived.	FORM: **had** = past participle
(c) He **'d** left. I **'d** left. They **'d** left. Etc.	CONTRACTION: I / you / she / he / it / we / they + **'d**
(d) Jack **had left** *before* Sue arrived. (e) Jack **left** *before* Sue arrived. (f) Sue **arrived** *after* Jack had left. (g) Sue **arrived** *after* Jack left.	When **before** and **after** are used in a sentence, the time relationship is already clear so the past perfect is often not necessary. The simple past may be used, as in (e) and (g). Examples (d) and (e) have the same meaning. Examples (f) and (g) have the same meaning.
(h) Stella was alone in a strange city. She walked down the avenue slowly, looking in shop windows. Suddenly, she turned her head and looked behind her. Someone **had called** her name.	The past perfect is more common in formal writing such as fiction, as in (h).

Chapter 5
Asking Questions

5-1 Yes/No Questions and Short Answers

Yes/No Question	Short Answer (+ Long Answer)	
(a) ***Do** you **like** tea?*	*Yes, I **do**.* (I like tea.) *No, I **don't**.* (I don't like tea.)	A **yes/no question** is a question that can be answered by *yes* or *no*.
(b) ***Did** Sue **call**?*	*Yes, she **did**.* (Sue called.) *No, she **didn't**.* (Sue didn't call.)	In an affirmative short answer (*yes*), a helping verb is NOT contracted with the subject.
(c) ***Have** you **met** Al?*	*Yes, I **have**.* (I have met Al.) *No, I **haven't**.* (I haven't met Al.)	In (c): *INCORRECT: Yes, I've.* In (d): *INCORRECT: Yes, it's.* In (e): *INCORRECT: Yes, he'll.*
(d) ***Is** it **raining**?*	*Yes, it **is**.* (It's raining.) *No, it **isn't**.* (It isn't raining.)	The spoken emphasis in a short answer is on the verb.
(e) ***Will** Rob **be** here?*	*Yes, he **will**.* (Rob will be here.) *No, he **won't**.* (Rob won't be here.)	

Q: ***Do** you **need** help?*
A: *Yes, I **do**.*

5-2 Yes/No and Information Questions

A yes/no question = a question that can be answered by "yes" or "no"
A: *Does Ann live in Montreal?*
B: *Yes, she does.* OR *No, she doesn't.*

An information question = a question that asks for information by using a question word:
where, when, why, who, whom, what, which, whose, how
A: *Where does Ann live?*
B: *In Montreal.*

(Question Word)	Helping Verb	Subject	Main Verb	(Rest of Sentence)	
(a)	*Does*	*Ann*	*live*	in Montreal?	The same subject-verb word order is used in both yes/no and information questions:
(b) Where	*does*	*Ann*	*live?*		*Helping Verb + Subject + Main Verb*
(c)	*Is*	*Sara*	*studying*	at the library?	
(d) Where	*is*	*Sara*	*studying?*		Example (a) is a yes/no question. Example (b) is an information question.
(e)	*Will*	*you*	*graduate*	next year?	
(f) When	*will*	*you*	*graduate?*		
(g)	*Did*	*they*	*see*	Jack?	
(h) Who(m)*	*did*	*they*	*see?*		In (i) and (j): Main verb **be** in simple present and simple past (**am, is, are, was, were**) precedes the subject. It has the same position as a helping verb.
(i)	*Is*	*Heidi*		at home?	
(j) Where	*is*	*Heidi?*			
(k)		*Who*	*came*	to dinner?	When the question word (e.g., **who** or **what**) is the subject of the question, usual question word order is not used. Notice in (k) and (l) that no form of **do** is used.
(l)		*What*	*happened*	yesterday?	

*See Chart 5-4 for a discussion of *who(m)*.

Q: Where *do Irena and Paul live?*
A: Near a lake.

5-3 Where, Why, When, What Time, How Come, What . . . For

Question	Answer	
(a) **Where** did he go?	Home.	**Where** asks about *place*.
(b) **When** did he leave?	Last night. Two days ago. Monday morning. Seven-thirty.	A question with **when** can be answered by any time expression, as in the sample answers in (b).
(c) **What time** did he leave?	Seven-thirty. Around five o'clock. A quarter past ten.	A question with **what time** asks about *time on a clock*.
(d) **Why** did he leave?	Because he didn't feel well.*	**Why** asks about *reason*.
(e) **What** did he leave *for*? (f) **How come** he left?	**Why** can also be expressed with the phrases **What . . . for** and **How come**, as in (e) and (f). Notice that with **How come**, usual question order is not used. The subject precedes the verb and no form of **do** is used.	

*See Chart 8-6, p. 62, for the use of *because*. *Because I didn't feel well* is an adverb clause. It is not a complete sentence. In this example, it is the short answer to a question.

5-4 Questions With Who, Who(m), and What

Question	Answer	
(a) **Who** came? (S)	**Someone** came. (S)	In (a): **Who** is used as the subject (S) of a question. In (b): **Who(m)** is used as the object (O) in a question.
(b) **Who(m)** did *you* see? (O)	I saw **someone**. (S) (O)	**Whom** is used in very formal English. In everyday spoken English, **who** is usually used instead of **whom**: UNCOMMON: Whom did you see? COMMON: Who did you see?
(c) **What** happened? (S)	**Something** happened. (S)	**What** can be used as either the subject or the object in a question.
(d) **What** did *you* see? (O)	I saw **something**. (S) (O)	Notice in (a) and (c): When **who** or **what** is used as the subject of a question, usual question word order is not used; no form of **do** is used: CORRECT: Who came? INCORRECT: Who did come?

5-5 Using *What* + a Form of *Do*

Question	Answer	
(a) What **does** Bob **do** every morning?	He *goes to class.*	**What** + a form of **do** is used to ask questions about activities.
(b) What **did** you **do** yesterday?	I *went downtown.*	
(c) What **is** Anna **doing** (right now)?	She*'s studying.*	Examples of forms of **do**: *am doing, will do, are going to do, did, etc.*
(d) What **are** you **going to do** tomorrow?	I*'m going to go to the beach.*	
(e) What **do** you **want to do** tonight?	I *want to go to a movie.*	
(f) What **would** you **like to do** tomorrow?	I *would like to visit Jim.*	

5-6 Using *Which* and *What Kind Of*

Which

(a) TOM: May I borrow a pen from you? ANN: Sure. I have two pens. This pen has black ink. That pen has red ink. **Which pen** do you want? OR **Which one** do you want? OR **Which** do you want?	In (a): Ann uses **which** (not **what**) because she wants Tom to choose. **Which** is used when the speaker wants someone to make a choice, when the speaker is offering alternatives: *this one or that one; these or those.*
(b) SUE: I like these earrings, and I like those too. BOB: **Which** (*earrings /ones*) are you going to buy? SUE: I think I'll get these.	**Which** can be used with either singular or plural nouns.
(c) JIM: Here's a photo of my daughter's class. KIM: Very nice. **Which one** is your daughter?	**Which** can be used to ask about people as well as things.
(d) SUE: My aunt gave me some money for my birthday. I'm going to take it with me to the mall. BOB: **What** are you going to buy with it? SUE: I haven't decided yet.	In (d): The question doesn't involve choosing from a particular group of items, so Bob uses **what**, not **which**.

What kind of

QUESTION	ANSWER	
(e) **What kind of** *shoes* did you buy?	Boots. Sandals. Tennis shoes. Loafers. Running shoes. High heels. Etc.	**What kind of** asks for information about a specific type (a specific kind) in a general category. In (e): general category = shoes specific kinds = boots sandals tennis shoes etc.
(f) **What kind of** *fruit* do you like best?	Apples. Bananas. Oranges. Grapefruit. Strawberries. Etc.	In (f): general category = fruit specific kinds = apples bananas oranges etc.

5-7 Using *Whose*

Question	Answer	
(a) *Whose* (*book*) is this?	It's John's (book).	*Whose* asks about possession.*
(b) *Whose* (*books*) are those?	They're mine (OR my books).	Notice in (a): The speaker of the question may omit the noun (*book*) if the meaning is clear to the listener.
(c) *Whose car* did you borrow?	I borrowed Karen's (car).	
COMPARE:		*Who's* and *whose* have the same pronunciation.
(d) *Who's* that?	Mary Smith.	*Who's* is a contraction of *who is*.
(e) *Whose* is that?	Mary's.	*Whose* asks about possession.

*See Charts 6-11, p. 44, and 6-12, p. 45, for ways of expressing possession.

5-8 Using *How*

Question	Answer	
(a) *How* did you get here?	I drove. / By car. I took a taxi. / By taxi. I took a bus. / By bus. I flew. / By plane. I took a train. / By train. I walked. / On foot.	*How* has many uses. One use of *how* is to ask about means (ways) of transportation.
(b) *How old* are you?	Twenty-one.	*How* is often used with adjectives (e.g., *old, big*) and adverbs (e.g., *well, quickly*).
(c) *How tall* is he?	About six feet.	
(d) *How big* is your apartment?	It has three rooms.	
(e) *How sleepy* are you?	Very sleepy.	
(f) *How hungry* are you?	I'm starving.	
(g) *How soon* will you be ready?	In five minutes.	
(h) *How well* does he speak English?	Very well.	
(i) *How quickly* can you get here?	I can get there in 30 minutes.	

5-9 Using *How Often*

Question	Answer	
(a) **How often** do you go shopping?	Every day. Once a week. About twice a week. Every other day or so.* Three times a month.	**How often** asks about frequency.
(b) **How many times a day** do you eat?	Three or four.	Other ways of asking **how often**:
How many times a week do you go shopping?	Two.	**how many times** { a day / a week / a month / a year
How many times a month do you go to the post office?	Once.	
How many times a year do you take a vacation?	Once or twice.	

Frequency Expressions

a lot	every	
occasionally	every other	
once in a while	once a	day / week / month / year
not very often	twice a	
hardly ever	three times a	
almost never	ten times a	
never		

Every other day means "Monday yes, Tuesday no, Wednesday yes, Thursday no," etc.
Or so means "approximately."

5-10 Using *How Far*

(a) **It is** 489 miles **from** Oslo **to** Helsinki by air.*	The most common way of expressing distance: **It is** + *distance* + **from/to** + **to/from**
(b) **It is** 3,605 miles { **from** Moscow **to** Beijing. **from** Beijing **to** Moscow. **to** Beijing **from** Moscow. **to** Moscow **from** Beijing.	In (b): All four expressions with **from** and **to** have the same meaning.
(c) — **How far is it** from Mumbai to Delhi? — 725 miles.	**How far** is used to ask questions about distance.
(d) — **How far do you** live from school? — Four blocks.	
(e) **How many miles** is it from London to Paris? (f) **How many kilometers** is it to Montreal from here? (g) **How many blocks** is it to the post office?	Other ways to ask **how far**: • *how many miles* • *how many kilometers* • *how many blocks*

*1 mile = 1.60 kilometers; 1 kilometer = 00.614 mile

5-11 Length of Time: *It* + *Take* and *How Long*

IT + TAKE + (SOMEONE) + LENGTH OF TIME + INFINITIVE					*It* + *take* is often used with time words and an infinitive to express **length of time**, as in (a) and (b).
(a)	*It*	takes		20 minutes	*to cook* rice.
(b)	*It*	took	Al	two hours	*to drive* to work.

It + *take* is often used with time words and an infinitive to express **length of time**, as in (a) and (b).

An infinitive = *to* + *the simple form of a verb.**

In (a): *to cook* is an infinitive.

(c) *How long* does it take to cook rice? Twenty minutes. (d) *How long* did it take Al to drive to work today? Two hours. (e) *How long* did you study last night? Four hours. (f) *How long* will you be in Hong Kong? Ten days.	*How long* asks about *length of time*.
(g) *How many days* will you be in Hong Kong?	Other ways of asking **how long**: *how many* + { minutes hours days weeks months years }

*See Chart 13-3, p. 92.

How long does it take to fly from London to Madrid?
About an hour and a half.

5-12 Spoken and Written Contractions with Question Words

Spoken Only

is	(a) "*When's* he coming?" "*Why's* she late?"	***Is*, *are*, *does*, *did*, *has*, *have***, and ***will*** are usually contracted with question words in speaking.
are	(b) "*What're* these?" "*Who're* they talking to?"	
does	(c) "*When's* the movie start?" "*Where's* he live?"	
did	(d) "*Who'd* you see?" "*What'd* you do?"	
has	(e) "*What's* she done?" "*Where's* he gone?"	
have	(f) "*How've* you been?" "*What've* I done?"	
will	(g) "*Where'll* you be?" "*When'll* they be here?"	
	(h) ***What do you*** → Whaddaya think? (i) ***What are you*** → Whaddaya thinking?	***What do you*** and ***What are you*** both can be reduced to "Whaddaya" in spoken English.

Written

is	(j) *Where's* Ed? *What's* that? *Who's* he?	Only contractions with ***where*, *what***, or ***who*** + ***is*** are commonly used in writing, such as in letters to friends or emails. They are generally not appropriate in more formal writing, such as in magazine articles or reference material.

When's Carlos coming back?

5-13 More Questions with *How*

Question	Answer	
(a) *How do you spell* "coming"? (b) *How do you say* "yes" in Japanese? (c) *How do you say / pronounce* this word?	C-O-M-I-N-G. Hai. ——	To answer (a): Spell the word. To answer (b): Say the word. To answer (c): Pronounce the word.
(d) *How are you getting along?* (e) *How are you doing?* (f) *How's it going?*	Great. Fine. Okay. So-so.	In (d), (e), and (f): How is your life? Is your life okay? Do you have any problems? NOTE: Example (f) is also used in greetings: *Hi, Bob. How's it going?*
(g) *How do you feel?* *How are you feeling?*	Terrific! Wonderful! Great! Fine. Okay. So-so. A bit under the weather. Not so good. Terrible! / Lousy. / Awful!	The questions in (g) ask about health or about general emotional state.
(h) *How do you do?*	How do you do?	*How do you do?* is used by two speakers when they meet each other for the first time in a somewhat formal situation, as in (h).★

★A: *Dr. Erickson, I'd like to introduce you to a friend of mine, Rick Brown. Rick, this is my biology professor, Dr. Erickson.*
B: ***How do you do,*** *Mr. Brown?*
C: ***How do you do,*** *Dr. Erickson? I'm pleased to meet you.*

5-14 Using *How About* and *What About*

(a) A: We need one more player. B: *How about/What about Jack?* Let's ask him if he wants to play.	*How about* and *what about* have the same meaning and usage. They are used to make suggestions or offers.
(b) A: What time should we meet? B: *How about/What about three o'clock?*	*How about* and *what about* are followed by a noun (or pronoun) or the *-ing* form of a verb (gerund).
(c) A: What should we do this afternoon? B: *How about going* to the zoo? (d) A: *What about asking* Sally over for dinner next Sunday? B: Okay. Good idea.	NOTE: *How about* and *what about* are frequently used in informal spoken English, but are usually not used in writing.
(e) A: I'm tired. *How about you?* B: Yes, I'm tired too. (f) A: Are you hungry? B: No. *What about you?* A: I'm a little hungry.	*How about you?* and *What about you?* are used to ask a question that refers to the information or question that immediately preceded it. In (e): *How about you?* = *Are you tired?* In (f): *What about you?* = *Are you hungry?*

5-15 Tag Questions

(a) Jill is sick, *isn't she?* (b) You didn't know, *did you?* (c) There's enough time, *isn't there?* (d) I'm not late, *am I?* (e) I'm late, *aren't I?*	A tag question is a question that is added onto the end of a sentence. An auxiliary verb is used in a tag question. Notice that *I am* becomes *aren't I* in a negative tag, as in (e). (*Am I not* is also possible, but it is very formal and rare.)

Affirmative (+)	Negative (−)	Affirmative Expected Answer	When the main verb is affirmative, the tag question is negative, and the expected answer agrees with the main verb.
(d) *You know* Bill,	*don't you?*	Yes.	
(e) *Marie is* from Paris,	*isn't she?*	Yes.	

Negative (−)	Affirmative (+)	Negative Expected Answer	When the main verb is negative, the tag question is affirmative, and the expected answer agrees with the main verb.
(f) *You don't know* Tom,	*do you?*	No.	
(g) *Marie isn't* from Athens,	*is she?*	No.	

THE SPEAKER'S QUESTION	THE SPEAKER'S IDEA
	Tag questions have two types of intonation: rising and falling. The intonation determines the meaning of the tag.
(h) It will be nice tomorrow, *won't it?*	A speaker uses rising intonation to make sure information is correct. In (h): the speaker has an idea; the speaker is checking to see if the idea is correct.
(i) It will be nice tomorrow, *won't it?*	Falling intonation is used when the speaker is seeking agreement. In (i): the speaker thinks it will be nice tomorrow and is almost certain the listener will agree.
YES/NO QUESTIONS (j) — Will it be nice tomorrow? — *Yes, it will.* OR *No, it won't.*	In (j): The speaker has no idea. The speaker is simply looking for information. Compare (h) and (i) with (j).

Chapter 6
Nouns and Pronouns

6-1 Plural Forms of Nouns

Singular	Plural	
(a) one bird one street one rose	two *birds* two *streets* two *roses*	To make most nouns plural, add *-s*.
(b) one dish one match one class one box	two *dishes* two *matches* two *classes* two *boxes*	Add *-es* to nouns ending in *-sh*, *-ch*, *-ss*, and *-x*.
(c) one baby one city	two *babies* two *cities*	If a noun ends in a consonant + *-y*, change the *y* to *i* and add *-es*, as in (c).
(d) one toy one key	two *toys* two *keys*	If *-y* is preceded by a vowel, add only *-s*, as in (d).
(e) one knife one shelf	two *knives* two *shelves*	If a noun ends in *-fe* or *-f*, change the ending to *-ves*. EXCEPTIONS: *beliefs, chiefs, roofs, cuffs, cliffs.*
(f) one tomato one zoo one zero	two *tomatoes* two *zoos* two *zeroes/zeros*	The plural form of nouns that end in *-o* is sometimes *-oes* and sometimes *-os*. *-oes*: tomatoes, potatoes, heroes, echoes *-os*: zoos, radios, studios, pianos, solos, sopranos, photos, autos, videos *-oes* or *-os*: zeroes/zeros, volcanoes/volcanos, tornadoes/tornados, mosquitoes/mosquitos
(g) one child one foot one goose one man one mouse one tooth one woman ————	two *children* two *feet* two *geese* two *men* two *mice* two *teeth* two *women* two *people*	Some nouns have irregular plural forms. NOTE: The singular form of *people* can be *person, woman, man, child*. For example, one *man* and one *child* = two *people*. (Two *persons* is also possible.)
(h) one deer one fish one sheep	two *deer* two *fish* two *sheep*	The plural form of some nouns is the same as the singular form.
(i) one bacterium one crisis	two *bacteria* two *crises*	Some nouns that English has borrowed from other languages have foreign plurals.

6-2 Pronunciation of Final -s/-es

Final **-s/-es** has three different pronunciations: /s/, /z/, and /əz/.

(a)	seats	=	seat/s/	Final **-s** is pronounced /s/ after voiceless sounds. In (a): /s/ is the sound of "s" in "bus."
	maps	=	map/s/	
	lakes	=	lake/s/	Examples of voiceless* sounds: /t/, /p/, /k/.

(b)	seeds	=	seed/z/	Final **-s** is pronounced /z/ after voiced sounds. In (b): /z/ is the sound of "z" in "buzz."
	stars	=	star/z/	
	holes	=	hole/z/	Examples of voiced* sounds: /d/, /r/, /l/, /m/, /b/, and all vowel sounds.
	laws	=	law/z/	

(c)	dishes	=	dish/əz/	Final **-s/-es** is pronounced /əz/ after -sh, -ch, -s, -z, -ge/-dge sounds.
	matches	=	match/əz/	In (c): /əz/ adds a syllable to a word.
	classes	=	class/əz/	
	sizes	=	size/əz/	
	pages	=	page/əz/	
	judges	=	judge/əz/	

*See Chart 2-5, p. 11, for more information about voiceless and voiced sounds.

6-3 Subjects, Verbs, and Objects

		S	V	An English sentence has a SUBJECT (S) and a VERB (V).
(a)	The	*sun*	*shines.*	The SUBJECT is a **noun**. In (a): *sun* is a noun; it is the subject of the verb *shines*.
		(noun)	(verb)	
		S	V	
(b)		*Plants*	*grow.*	
		(noun)	(verb)	

		S	V	O	
(c)		*Plants*	*need*	*water.*	Sometimes a VERB is followed by an OBJECT (O).
		(noun)	(verb)	(noun)	The OBJECT of a verb is a **noun**. In (c): *water* is the object of the verb *need*.
		S	V	O	
(d)		*Bob*	*is reading*	*a book.*	
		(noun)	(verb)	(noun)	

6-4 Objects of Prepositions

S V O PREP O OF PREP (a) Ann put her books **on** *the* **desk**. (noun)	Many English sentences have prepositional phrases. In (a): **on the desk** is a prepositional phrase. A prepositional phrase consists of a PREPOSITION (PREP) and an OBJECT OF A PREPOSITION (O of PREP). The object of a preposition is a NOUN.
S V PREP O OF PREP (b) A leaf fell **to** *the* **ground**. (noun)	

Reference List of Prepositions

about	before	despite	of	to
above	behind	down	off	toward(s)
across	below	during	on	under
after	beneath	for	out	until
against	beside	from	over	up
along	besides	in	since	upon
among	between	into	through	with
around	beyond	like	throughout	within
at	by	near	till	without

6-5 Prepositions of Time

in	(a) Please be on time *in the future*. (b) I usually watch TV *in the evening*.	*in* + *the past, the present, the future** *in* + *the morning, the afternoon, the evening*
	(c) I was born *in October*. (d) I was born *in 1995*. (e) I was born *in the 20th century*. (f) The weather is hot *in* (the) *summer*.	*in* + { *a month* *a year* *a century* *a season* }
on	(g) I was born *on October 31st, 1995*. (h) I went to a movie *on Thursday*. (i) I have class *on Thursday morning(s)*.	*on* + a date *on* + a weekday *on* + (a) weekday morning(s), afternoon(s), evening(s)
at	(j) We sleep at night. I was asleep *at midnight*. (k) I fell asleep *at 9:30* (nine-thirty). (l) He's busy *at the moment*. Can I take a message?	*at* + *noon, night, midnight* *at* + "clock time" *at* + *the moment, the present time, present*

*Possible in British English: *in future* (e.g., *Please be on time in future.*).

6-6 Word Order: Place and Time

(a) Ann moved *to Paris in 2008*. We went *to a movie yesterday*. S V PLACE TIME	In a typical English sentence, "place" comes before "time," as in (a). *INCORRECT: Ann moved in 2008 to Paris.*
(b) We bought a house in Miami in 2005. S V O P T	S-V-O-P-T = Subject-Verb-Object-Place-Time (basic English sentence structure)
(c) *In 2008,* Ann moved to Paris. TIME S V PLACE (d) *Yesterday* we went to a movie.	Expressions of time can also come at the beginning of a sentence, as in (c) and (d). A time phrase at the beginning of a sentence is often followed by a comma, as in (c).

6-7 Subject-Verb Agreement

(a) The *sun* shine*s*. SINGULAR SINGULAR (b) *Birds sing*. PLURAL PLURAL	A singular subject takes a singular verb, as in (a). A plural subject takes a plural verb, as in (b). Notice: *verb* + *-s* = singular (*shines*) *noun* + *-s* = plural (*birds*)
(c) *My brother* **lives** in Jakarta. SINGULAR SINGULAR (d) *My brother* **and** *sister* **live** in Jakarta. PLURAL PLURAL	Two subjects connected by **and** take a plural verb, as in (d).
(e) The **glasses** over there under the window by the sink **are** clean. (f) The **information** in those magazines about Vietnamese culture and customs **is** very interesting.	Sometimes phrases come between a subject and a verb. These phrases do not affect the agreement of the subject and verb.
(g) *There* **is** *a* **book** on the desk. V S (h) *There* **are** *some* **books** on the desk. V S	**There** + **be** + *subject* expresses that something exists in a particular place. The verb agrees with the noun that follows **be**.
(i) **Every student is** sitting down. (j) **Everybody/Everyone hopes** for peace.	**Every** is a singular word. It is used with a singular, not plural, noun. *INCORRECT: Every students . . .* Subjects with **every** take singular verbs, as in (i) and (j).
(k) **People** in my country **are** friendly.	**People** is a plural noun and takes a plural verb.

6-8 · Using Adjectives to Describe Nouns

ADJECTIVE NOUN (a) Bob is reading a **good** book.	Words that describe nouns are called ADJECTIVES. In (a): **good** is an adjective; it describes the book.
(b) The **tall** woman wore a **new** dress. (c) The **short** woman wore an **old** dress. (d) The **young** woman wore a **short** dress.	We say that adjectives "modify" nouns. *Modify* means "change a little." An adjective changes the meaning of a noun by giving more information about it.
(e) Roses are **beautiful** flowers. *INCORRECT: Roses are beautifuls flowers.*	Adjectives are neither singular nor plural. They do NOT have a plural form.
(f) He wore a **white** shirt. *INCORRECT: He wore a shirt white.* (g) Roses are **beautiful.** (h) His shirt was **white.**	Adjectives usually come immediately before nouns, as in (f). Adjectives can also follow main verb **be**, as in (g) and (h).

6-9 Using Nouns as Adjectives

(a) I have a **flower** garden. (b) The **shoe** store also sells socks.	Sometimes words that are usually used as nouns are used as adjectives. For example, **flower** is usually a noun, but in (a), it's used as an adjective to modify **garden**.
(c) *INCORRECT: a flowers garden* (d) *INCORRECT: the shoes store*	When a noun is used as an adjective, it is singular in form, NOT plural.

Jon climbs *mountains.*
He is a *mountain climber.*

6-10 Personal Pronouns: Subjects and Objects

Personal Pronouns

SUBJECT PRONOUNS:	*I*	*we*	*you*	*he, she, it*	*they*
OBJECT PRONOUNS:	*me*	*us*	*you*	*him, her, it*	*them*

(a) *Kate* is married. *She* has two children. S	A pronoun refers to a noun. In (a): *she* is a pronoun; it refers to *Kate*. In (b): *her* is a pronoun; it refers to *Kate*.
(b) *Kate* is my friend. I know *her* well. O	In (a): *She* is a SUBJECT PRONOUN. In (b): *her* is an OBJECT PRONOUN.
(c) Mike has *a new blue bike*. He bought *it* yesterday.	A pronoun can refer to a single noun (e.g., *Kate*) or to a noun phrase. In (c): *it* refers to the whole noun phrase *a new blue bike*.
(d) *Eric and I* are good friends. S	Guidelines for using pronouns following *and*: If the pronoun is used as part of the subject, use a subject pronoun, as in (d).
(e) Ann met *Eric and me* at the museum. O	If the pronoun is part of the object, use an object pronoun, as in (e) and (f).
(f) Ann walked between *Eric and me*. O of PREP	INCORRECT: *Eric and me are good friends.* INCORRECT: *Ann met Eric and I at the museum.*

SINGULAR PRONOUNS:	*I*	*me*	*you*	*he, she, it*	*him, her*
PLURAL PRONOUNS:	*we*	*us*	*you*	*they*	*them*

(g) *Mike* is in class. *He* is taking a test.	Singular = one. Plural = more than one.
(h) The *students* are in class. *They* are taking a test.	Singular pronouns refer to singular nouns; plural pronouns refer to plural nouns, as in the examples.
(i) *Kate and Tom* are married. *They* have two children.	

Kate and Tom are married.
They have two children.

6-11 Possessive Nouns

SINGULAR:	(a) I know the *student's* name.	An apostrophe (') and an **-s** are used with nouns to show possession.
PLURAL:	(b) I know the *students'* names.	
PLURAL:	(c) I know the *children's* names.	

SINGULAR	(d)	the student my baby a man	→ → →	the *student's* name my *baby's* name a *man's* name
				SINGULAR POSSESSIVE NOUN: *noun* + *apostrophe* (') + **-s**
	(e)	James	→	*James'/James's* name
				A singular noun that ends in **-s** has two possible possessive forms: *James'* OR *James's*.
PLURAL	(f)	the students my babies	→ →	the *students'* names my *babies'* names
				PLURAL POSSESSIVE NOUN: *noun* + **-s** + *apostrophe* (')
	(g)	men the children	→ →	*men's* names the *children's* names
				IRREGULAR PLURAL POSSESSIVE NOUN: *noun* + *apostrophe* (') + **-s** (An irregular plural noun is a plural noun that does not end in **-s**: *children, men, people, women.* See Chart 6-1.)
Compare: (h) *Tom's* here. (i) *Tom's* brother is here.				In (h): *Tom's* is not a possessive noun. It is a contraction of *Tom is,* used in informal writing. In (i): *Tom's* is a possessive noun.

the *teachers'* office.

the *teacher's* office.

6-12 Possessive Pronouns and Adjectives

This pen belongs to me. (a) It's **mine**. (b) It is **my** pen.		Examples (a) and (b) have the same meaning; they both show possession. **Mine** is a *possessive pronoun;* **my** is a *possessive adjective.*
POSSESSIVE PRONOUNS (c) I have **mine**. (d) You have **yours**. (e) She has **hers**. (f) He has **his**. (g) We have **ours**. (h) You have **yours**. (i) They have **theirs**. (j) ————	POSSESSIVE ADJECTIVES I have **my** pen. You have **your** pen. She has **her** pen. He has **his** pen. We have **our** pens. You have **your** pen. They have **their** pens. I have a book. **Its** cover is black.	A POSSESSIVE PRONOUN is used alone, without a noun following it. A POSSESSIVE ADJECTIVE is used only with a noun following it. INCORRECT: *I have mine pen.* INCORRECT: *I have my.*
COMPARE **its** VS. **it's**: (k) Sue gave me a book. I don't remember **its** title. (l) Sue gave me a book. **It's** a novel.		In (k): **its** (NO apostrophe) is a possessive adjective modifying the noun *title.* In (l): **It's** (with an apostrophe) is a contraction of *it + is.*

COMPARE **their** vs. **there** vs. **they're**:
(m) The students have **their** books.
(n) My books are over **there**.
(o) Where are the students? **They're** in class.
		Their, there, and **they're** have the same pronunciation, but not the same meaning.
		  their = possessive adjective, as in (m)
		  there = an expression of place, as in (n)
		  they're = *they are,* as in (o)

Nina and Rita are joining *their* friends for dinner tonight.

6-13 Reflexive Pronouns

		Reflexive pronouns end in **-self/-selves**. They are used when the subject (e.g., *I*) and the object (e.g., *myself*) are the same person.
myself	(a) *I* saw **myself** in the mirror.	
yourself	(b) *You* (one person) saw **yourself**.	
herself	(c) *She* saw **herself**.	
himself	(d) *He* saw **himself**.	*INCORRECT: I saw me in the mirror.*
itself	(e) *It* (e.g., the kitten) saw **itself**.	
ourselves	(f) *We* saw **ourselves**.	
yourselves	(g) *You* (plural) saw **yourselves**.	
themselves	(h) *They* saw **themselves**.	

(i) *Greg* lives **by himself**.	**By** + *a reflexive pronoun* = alone
(j) *I* sat **by myself** on the park bench.	In (i): Greg lives alone, without family or roommates.
(k) *I* **enjoyed myself** at the fair.	*Enjoy* and a few other verbs are commonly followed by a reflexive pronoun. See the list below.

Common Expressions with Reflexive Pronouns

believe in yourself	help yourself	pinch yourself	tell yourself
blame yourself	hurt yourself	be proud of yourself	work for yourself
cut yourself	give yourself (something)	take care of yourself	wish yourself (luck)
enjoy yourself	introduce yourself	talk to yourself	
feel sorry for yourself	kill yourself	teach yourself	

6-14 Singular Forms of *Other: Another* vs. *The Other*

Another

(a) There is a large bowl of apples on the table. Paul is going to eat one apple. If he is still hungry after that, he can eat ***another*** apple. There are many apples to choose from.	**Another** means "one more out of a group of similar items, one in addition to the one(s) already mentioned." **Another** is a combination of *an + other*, written as one word.

The Other

(b) There are two apples on the table. Paul is going to eat one of them. Sara is going to eat ***the other*** apple.	**The other** means "the last one in a specific group; the only one that remains from a given number of similar items."
(c) Paul ate one apple. Then he ate { ***another*** apple. ***another*** one. ***another***.	**Another** and ***the other*** can be used as adjectives in front of a noun (e.g., *apple*) or in front of the word *one*. **Another** and ***the other*** can also be used alone as pronouns.
(d) Paul ate one apple. Sara ate { ***the other*** apple. ***the other*** one. ***the other***.	

6-15 Plural Forms of *Other*: *Other(s)* vs. *The Other(s)*

Other(s)

There are many apples in Paul's kitchen. Paul is holding one apple.	**Other(s)** (without **the**) means "several more out of a group of similar items, several in addition to the one(s) already mentioned."
(a) There are ***other*** *apples* in a bowl. (adjective) + (noun)	The adjective ***other*** (without an **-s**) can be used with a plural noun (e.g., *apples*) or with the word ***ones***.
(b) There are ***other*** *ones* on a plate. (adjective) + *ones*	***Others*** (with an **-s**) is a plural pronoun; it is not used with a noun.
(c) There are ***others*** on a chair. (pronoun)	In (c): ***others*** = ***other apples***

The Other(s)

There are four apples on the table. Paul is going to take one of them.	***The other(s)*** means "the last ones in a specific group, the remains from a given number of similar items."
(d) Sara is going to take ***the other*** *apples.* (adjective) + (noun)	***The other*** (without an **-s**) can be used as an adjective in front of a noun or the word ***ones***, as in (d) and (e).
(e) Sara is going to take ***the other*** *ones.* (adjective) + *ones*	***The others*** (with an **-s**) is a plural pronoun; it is not used with a noun.
(f) Sara is going to take ***the others.*** (pronoun)	In (f): ***the others*** = ***the other apples***

6-16 Summary of Forms of *Other*

	Adjective	Pronoun	
SINGULAR	another apple	another	Notice that the word ***others*** (***other*** + *final* **-s**) is used only as a plural pronoun.
PLURAL	other apples	other**s**	
SINGULAR	the other apple	the other	
PLURAL	the other apples	the other**s**	

Two trees are taller than *the others*.

Chapter 7
Modal Auxiliaries

7-1 The Form of Modal Auxiliaries

The verbs listed below are called "modal auxiliaries." They are helping verbs that express a wide range of meanings (ability, permission, possibility, necessity, etc.). Most of the modals have more than one meaning.

Auxiliary + the Simple Form of a Verb

can	(a) Olga *can speak* English.	*Can, could, may, might, should, had better, must, will,* and *would* are immediately followed by the simple form of a verb.
could	(b) He *couldn't come* to class.	
may	(c) It *may rain* tomorrow.	
might	(d) It *might rain* tomorrow.	• They are not followed by *to*.
should	(e) Mary *should study* harder.	*INCORRECT: Olga can to speak English.*
had better	(f) I *had better study* tonight.	• The main verb does not have a final *-s*.
must	(g) Billy! You *must listen* to me!	*INCORRECT: Olga can speaks English.*
will	(h) I *will be* in class tomorrow.	• The main verb is not in a past form.
would	(i) *Would* you please *close* the door?	*INCORRECT: Olga can spoke English.*
		• The main verb is not in its *-ing* form.
		INCORRECT: Olga can speaking English.

Auxiliary + *to* + the Simple Form of a Verb

have to	(j) I *have to study* tonight.	*To* + *the simple form* is used with these auxiliaries: *have to, have got to, be able to,* and *ought to.*
have got to	(k) I *have got to study* tonight.	
be able to	(l) Kate *is able to study* harder.	
ought to	(m) Kate *ought to study* harder.	

7-2 Expressing Ability: *Can* and *Could*

(a) Bob *can play* the piano. (b) You *can buy* a screwdriver at a hardware store. (c) I *can meet* you at Ted's tomorrow afternoon.	*Can* expresses *ability* in the present or future.
(d) I $\left\{\begin{array}{l} \textit{can't} \\ \textit{cannot} \\ \textit{can not} \end{array}\right\}$ understand that sentence.	The negative form of *can* may be written *can't*, *cannot*, or *can not*.
(e) I can gó. (f) I cán't go.	In spoken English, *can* is usually unstressed and pronounced /kən/ = "kun." *Can't* is stressed and pronounced /kæn?/, with the final sound being a glottal stop.* The glottal stop replaces the /t/ in spoken English. Occasionally native speakers have trouble hearing the difference between *can* and *can't* and have to ask for clarification.
(g) Our son *could walk* when he was one year old.	The past form of *can* is *could*.
(h) He *couldn't walk* when he was six months old.	The negative of *could* is *couldn't* or *could not*.
(i) He *can read*. (j) He *is able to read*. (k) She *could read*. (l) She *was able to read*.	Ability can also be expressed with a form of *be able to*. Examples (i) and (j) have the same meaning. Examples (k) and (l) have the same meaning.

*A glottal stop is the sound you hear in the negative "unh-uh." The air is stopped by the closing of your glottis in the back of your throat. The phonetic symbol for the glottal stop is /ʔ/.

Bears *can survive* the winter without food.

7-3 Expressing Possibility: *May, Might,* and *Maybe;* Expressing Permission: *May* and *Can*

(a) It *may rain* tomorrow. (b) It *might rain* tomorrow. (c) — Why isn't John in class? — I don't know. He { *may* / *might* } be sick today.	*May* and *might* express *possibility* in the present or future. They have the same meaning. There is no difference in meaning between (a) and (b).
(d) It *may not rain* tomorrow. (e) It *might not rain* tomorrow.	Negative: *may not* and *might not* (Do not contract *may* and *might* with *not*.)
(f) *Maybe* it will rain tomorrow. COMPARE: (g) *Maybe* John is sick. (*adverb*) (h) John *may be* sick. (*verb*)	In (f) and (g): *maybe* (spelled as one word) is an adverb. It means "possibly." It comes at the beginning of a sentence. INCORRECT: It will maybe rain tomorrow. In (h): *may be* (two words) is a verb form: the auxiliary *may* + the main verb *be*. Examples (g) and (h) have the same meaning. INCORRECT: John maybe sick.
(i) Yes, children, you *may have* a cookie after dinner. (j) Okay, kids, you *can have* a cookie after dinner.	*May* is also used to give *permission*, as in (i). *Can* is often used to give *permission*, too, as in (j). NOTE: Examples (i) and (j) have the same meaning, but *may* is more formal than *can*.
(k) You *may not have* a cookie. You *can't have* a cookie.	*May not* and *cannot* (*can't*) are used to deny permission (i.e., to say "no").

7-4 Using *Could* to Express Possibility

(a) — How was the movie? *Could* you *understand* the English? — Not very well. I *could* only *understand* it with the help of subtitles.	One meaning of *could* is *past ability,* as in (a).* Another meaning of *could* is *possibility.* In (b): *He could be sick* has the same meaning as *He may/might be sick,* i.e., *It is possible that he is sick.*
(b) — Why isn't Greg in class? — I don't know. He *could be* sick.	In (b): *could* expresses a *present* possibility.
(c) Look at those dark clouds. It *could start* raining any minute.	In (c): *could* expresses a *future* possibility.

*See also Chart 7-2.

7-5 Polite Questions: *May I, Could I, Can I*

Polite Question	Possible Answers	
(a) *May I* please borrow your pen? (b) *Could I* please borrow your pen? (c) *Can I* please borrow your pen?	Yes. Yes. Of course. Yes. Certainly. Of course. Certainly. Sure. (*informal*) Okay. (*informal*) Uh-huh (*meaning "yes"*) I'm sorry, but I need to use it myself.	People use *may I*, *could I*,* and *can I* to ask polite questions. The questions ask for someone's permission or agreement. Examples (a), (b), and (c) have basically the same meaning. NOTE: *can I* is less formal than *may I* and *could I*.
(d) *Can I* borrow your pen, *please*? (e) *Can I* borrow your pen?		*Please* can come at the end of the question, as in (d). *Please* can be omitted from the question, as in (e).

*In a polite question, *could* is NOT the past form of *can*.

7-6 Polite Questions: *Would You, Could You, Will You, Can You*

Polite Question	Possible Answers	
(a) *Would you* please open the door? (b) *Could you* please open the door? (c) *Will you* please open the door? (d) *Can you* please open the door?	Yes. Yes. Of course. Certainly. I'd be happy to. Of course. I'd be glad to. Sure. (informal) Okay. (informal) Uh-huh. (meaning "yes") I'm sorry. I'd like to help, but my hands are full.	People use *would you*, *could you*, *will you*, and *can you* to ask polite questions. The questions ask for someone's help or cooperation. Examples (a), (b), (c), and (d) have basically the same meaning. *Would* and *could* are generally considered more polite than *will* and *can*.
		NOTE: *May* is NOT used when *you* is the subject of a polite question. *INCORRECT:* May you please open the door?

7-7 Expressing Advice: *Should* and *Ought To*

(a) My clothes are dirty. I $\left\{\begin{array}{l}\textit{should}\\\textit{ought to}\end{array}\right\}$ wash them.	**Should** and **ought to** have the same meaning: "This is a good idea. This is good advice."

(b) INCORRECT: *I should to wash them.*
(c) INCORRECT: *I ought washing them.*
	FORMS:
	    should + *simple form of a verb* (no **to**)
	    ought + **to** + *simple form of a verb*

(d) You need your sleep. You *should not* (*shouldn't*) stay up late.	NEGATIVE: **should** + **not** = **shouldn't** (*Ought to* is usually not used in the negative.)
(e) A: I'm going to be late for the bus. What *should I do?* B: Run!	QUESTION: **should** + *subject* + *main verb* (*Ought to* is usually not used in questions.)
(f) A: I'm tired today. B: You *should/ought to* go home and take a nap.	The use of **maybe** with **should** and **ought to** "softens" advice.
(g) A: I'm tired today. B: *Maybe* you *should/ought to* go home and take a nap.	COMPARE: In (f): Speaker B is giving definite advice. He is stating clearly that he believes going home for a nap is a good idea and is the solution to Speaker A's problem. In (g): Speaker B is making a suggestion: going home for a nap is one possible way to solve Speaker A's problem.

7-8 Expressing Advice: *Had Better*

(a) My clothes are dirty. I $\left\{\begin{array}{l}\textit{should}\\\textit{ought to}\\\textit{had better}\end{array}\right\}$ *wash* them.	**Had better** has the same basic meaning as *should* and *ought to*: "This is a good idea. This is good advice."
(b) You're driving too fast! You*'d better slow* down.	**Had better** has more of a sense of urgency than *should* or *ought to*. It often implies a warning about possible bad consequences. In (b): If you don't slow down, there could be a bad result. You could get a speeding ticket or have an accident.
(c) You*'d better not eat* that meat. It looks spoiled.	NEGATIVE: **had better not**
(d) I*'d better send* my boss an email right away.	In conversation, **had** is usually contracted: *'d*.

7-9 Expressing Necessity: *Have to, Have Got to, Must*

(a) I have a very important test tomorrow. I $\left\{\begin{array}{l}\textit{have to}\\\textit{have got to}\\\textit{must}\end{array}\right\}$ *study* tonight.	**Have to**, **have got to**, and **must** have basically the same meaning. They express the idea that something is necessary.
(b) I'd like to go with you to the movie this evening, but I can't. I **have to go** to a meeting. (c) Bye now! I**'ve got to go**. My wife's waiting for me. I'll call you later. (d) All passengers *must present* their passports at customs upon arrival. (e) Tommy, you *must hold* onto the railing when you go down the stairs.	**Have to** is used much more frequently in everyday speech and writing than **must**. **Have got to** is typically used in informal conversation, as in (c). **Must** is typically found in written instructions or rules, as in (d). Adults also use it when talking to younger children, as in (e). It sounds very strong.
(f) *Do* we **have to bring** pencils to the test? (g) Why *did* he **have to leave** so early?	QUESTIONS: **Have to** is usually used in questions, not **must** or **have got to**. Forms of **do** are used with **have to** in questions.
(h) I **had to** *study* last night.	The PAST form of **have to**, **have got to**, and **must** (meaning necessity) is **had to**.
(i) I **have to** ("hafta") *go* downtown today. (j) Rita **has to** ("hasta") *go* to the bank. (k) I've **got to** ("gotta") *study* tonight.	Notice that **have to**, **has to**, and **have got to** are commonly reduced, as in (i) through (k).

7-10 Expressing Lack of Necessity: *Do Not Have To;* Expressing Prohibition: *Must Not*

(a) I finished all of my homework this afternoon. I **don't have to study** tonight. (b) Tomorrow is a holiday. Mary **doesn't have to go** to class.	**Don't / doesn't have to** expresses the idea that something is *not necessary*.
(c) Bus passengers **must not talk** to the driver. (d) Children, you **must not play** with matches!	**Must not** expresses *prohibition* (DO NOT DO THIS!).
(e) You **mustn't play** with matches.	**Must + not = mustn't** (NOTE: The first "t" is not pronounced.)

7-11 Making Logical Conclusions: *Must*

(a) A: Nancy is yawning. B: She *must be* sleepy.	In (a): Speaker B is making a logical guess. He bases his guess on the information that Nancy is yawning. His logical conclusion, his "best guess," is that Nancy is sleepy. He uses *must* to express his logical conclusion.
(b) LOGICAL CONCLUSION: Amy plays tennis every day. She *must like* to play tennis. (c) NECESSITY: If you want to get into the movie theater, you *must buy* a ticket.	COMPARE: **Must** can express • a logical conclusion, as in (b). • necessity, as in (c).
(d) NEGATIVE LOGICAL CONCLUSION: Eric ate everything on his plate except the pickle. He *must not like* pickles. (e) PROHIBITION: There are sharks in the ocean near our hotel. We *must not go* swimming there.	COMPARE: **Must not** can express • a negative logical conclusion, as in (d). • prohibition, as in (e).

7-12 Tag Questions with Modal Auxiliaries

(a) You *can* come, *can't you*? (b) She *won't* tell, *will she*? (c) He *should* help, *shouldn't he*? (d) They *couldn't* do it, *could they*? (e) We *would like* to help, *wouldn't we*?	Tag questions are common with these modal auxiliaries: *can*, *will*, *should*, *could*, and *would*.*
(f) They *have to leave*, *don't they*? (g) They *don't have to leave*, *do they*? (h) He *has to leave*, *doesn't he*? (i) He *doesn't have to leave*, *does he*? (j) You *had to leave*, *didn't you*? (k) You *didn't have to leave*, *did you*?	Tag questions are also common with *have to*, *has to*, and *had to*. Notice that forms of *do* are used for the tag in (f) through (k).

*See Chart 5-15, p. 37, for information on how to use tag questions.

7-13 Giving Instructions: Imperative Sentences

COMMAND:
(a) Captain: *Open* the door!
   Soldier: Yes, sir!
 	
REQUEST:
(b) Teacher: *Open* the door, please.
   Student: Sure.
 	
DIRECTIONS:
(c) Barbara: Could you tell me how to get to the post office?
   Stranger: Certainly. *Walk* two blocks down this street. *Turn* left and *walk* three more blocks. It's on the right-hand side of the street.
	Imperative sentences are used to give commands, make polite requests, and give directions. The difference between a command and a request lies in the speaker's tone of voice and the use of *please*.
	
	Please can come at the beginning or end of a request:
	   Open the door, please.
	   Please open the door.

(d) *Close* the window. (e) Please *sit* down. (f) *Be* quiet! (g) *Don't walk* on the grass. (h) Please *don't wait* for me. (i) *Don't be* late.	The simple form of a verb is used in imperative sentences. In (d): The understood subject of the sentence is *you* (meaning the person the speaker is talking to): *Close the window = You close the window.* NEGATIVE FORM: *Don't* + *the simple form of a verb*

7-14 Making Suggestions: *Let's* and *Why Don't*

(a) — It's hot today. *Let's* go to the beach.
   — Okay. Good idea.
 	
(b) — It's hot today. *Why don't we* go to the beach?
   — Okay. Good idea.
	Let's and *Why don't we* are used to make suggestions about activities for you and another person to do.
	Examples (a) and (b) have the same meaning.
	Let's = *let us*

(c) — I'm tired.
   — *Why don't you* take a nap?
   — That's a good idea. I think I will.
	In (c): *Why don't you* is used to make a friendly suggestion or to give friendly advice.

7-15 Stating Preferences: *Prefer, Like . . . Better, Would Rather*

(a) I *prefer* apples *to* oranges. (b) I *prefer* watching TV *to* studying.	***prefer*** + *noun* + ***to*** + *noun* ***prefer*** + ***-ing*** verb + ***to*** + ***-ing*** verb
(c) I *like* apples *better than* oranges. (d) I *like* watching TV *better than* studying.	***like*** + *noun* + ***better than*** + *noun* ***like*** + ***-ing*** verb + ***better than*** + ***-ing*** verb
(e) Ann *would rather have* an apple than an orange. (f) INCORRECT: *Ann would rather has an apple.* (g) I'd rather visit a big city *than live* there. (h) INCORRECT: *I'd rather visit a big city than to live there.* INCORRECT: *I'd rather visit a big city than living there.*	***Would rather*** is followed immediately by the simple form of a verb (e.g., *have, visit, live*), as in (e). Verbs following ***than*** are also in the simple form, as in (g).
(i) *I'd / You'd / She'd / He'd / We'd / They'd* rather have an apple.	Contraction of ***would*** = ***'d***
(j) *Would you rather* have an apple *or* an orange?	In (j): In a polite question, ***would rather*** can be followed by *or* to offer someone a choice.

James and his family *prefer* skiing *to* ice skating.

Chapter 8
Connecting Ideas

8-1 Connecting Ideas with *And*

Connecting Items within a Sentence

(a) NO COMMA: I saw a cat **and** a mouse. (b) COMMAS: I saw a cat**,** a mouse**,** *and* a dog.	When **and** connects only TWO WORDS (or phrases) within a sentence, NO COMMA is used, as in (a). When **and** connects THREE OR MORE items within a sentence, COMMAS are used, as in (b).*

Connecting Two Sentences

(c) COMMA: I saw a cat**,** *and* you saw a mouse.	When **and** connects TWO COMPLETE SENTENCES (also called "independent" clauses), a COMMA is usually used, as in (c).
(d) PERIOD: I saw a cat**.** **Y**ou saw a mouse. (e) *INCORRECT: I saw a cat, you saw a mouse.*	Without **and**, two complete sentences are separated by a period, as in (d), *not* a comma.** A complete sentence begins with a capital letter; note that *You* is capitalized in (d).

*In a series of three or more items, the comma before **and** is optional.
      ALSO CORRECT: *I saw a cat, a mouse and a dog.*

**A "period" (the dot used at the end of a sentence) is called a "full stop" in British English.

A giraffe has a long neck *and* a short tail.

8-2 Connecting Ideas with *But* and *Or*

(a) I *went* to bed *but couldn't sleep.* (b) Is a lemon *sweet or sour?* (c) Did you order *coffee, tea, or milk?*	***And, but,*** and ***or*** are called "coordinating conjunctions." Like ***and, but*** and ***or*** can connect items within a sentence. Commas are used with a series of three or more items, as in (c).
I dropped the vase. = a sentence *It didn't break.* = a sentence (d) I dropped the vase, *but* it didn't break. (e) Do we have class on Monday, *or* is Monday a holiday?	A comma is usually used when ***but*** or ***or*** combines two complete (independent) sentences into one sentence, as in (d) and (e). A conjunction can also come at the beginning of a sentence, except in formal writing. ALSO CORRECT: I dropped the vase. But it didn't break. I saw a cat. And you saw a mouse.

8-3 Connecting Ideas with *So*

(a) The room was dark, *so* I turned on a light.	***So*** can be used as a conjunction, as in (a). It is preceded by a comma. It connects the ideas in two independent clauses.
	
	So expresses **results**:
	     cause: *The room was dark.*
	     result: *I turned on a light.*

(b) COMPARE: The room was dark, *but* I didn't turn on a light.	***But*** often expresses an unexpected result, as in (b).

8-4 Using Auxiliary Verbs after *But*

(a) I *don't like* coffee, but my husband *does.*
(b) I *like* tea, but my husband *doesn't.*
(c) I *won't be* here tomorrow, but Sue *will.*
(d) I*'ve seen* that movie, but Joe *hasn't.*
(e) He *isn't* here, but she *is.**
	After ***but***, often only an auxiliary verb is used. It has the same tense or modal as the main verb.
	
	In (a): ***does*** = likes coffee
	
	Notice in the examples:
	     negative + ***but*** *+ affirmative*
	     affirmative + ***but*** *+ negative*

*A verb is not contracted with a pronoun at the end of a sentence after ***but*** and ***and***:
     CORRECT: . . . *but she is.*
     INCORRECT: . . . *but she's.*

8-5 Using *And* + *Too, So, Either, Neither*

<table>
<tr>
<td>

                  S + AUX + *TOO*

(a) Sue works, *and* **Tom does too**.

               SO + AUX + S

(b) Sue works, *and* **so   does Tom**.

</td>
<td>

In affirmative statements, an auxiliary verb + **too** or **so** can be used after **and**.

Examples (a) and (b) have the same meaning.

Word order:

   subject + *auxiliary* + **too**

   so   + *auxiliary* + *subject*

</td>
</tr>
<tr>
<td>

               S + AUX + *EITHER*

(c) Ann doesn't work, *and* **Joe doesn't either**.

           NEITHER + AUX + S

(d) Ann doesn't work, *and* **neither does Joe**.

</td>
<td>

An auxiliary verb + **either** or **neither** are used with negative statements.

Examples (c) and (d) have the same meaning.

Word order:

   subject + *auxiliary* + **either**

   neither + *auxiliary* + *subject*

NOTE: An affirmative auxiliary is used with *neither*.

</td>
</tr>
<tr>
<td>

(e) — I'm hungry.

      — ***I am too.* / *So am I.***

(f) — I don't eat meat.

      — ***I don't either.* / *Neither do I.***

</td>
<td>

And is not usually used when there are two speakers.

</td>
</tr>
<tr>
<td>

(g) — I'm hungry.

      — ***Me too.*** (*informal*)

(h) — I don't eat meat.

      — ***Me (n)either.*** (*informal*)

</td>
<td>

Me too, **me either**, and **me neither** are often used in informal spoken English.

</td>
</tr>
</table>

The drivers in front of me have to pay a toll, *and so do I*.

8-6 Connecting Ideas with *Because*

(a) He drank water *because* he was thirsty.	***Because*** expresses a cause; it gives a reason. Why did he drink water? *Reason:* He was thirsty.
(b) MAIN CLAUSE: *He drank water.*	A main clause is a complete sentence: ***He drank water*** = a complete sentence
(c) ADVERB CLAUSE: *because he was thirsty*	An adverb clause is NOT a complete sentence: ***because he was thirsty*** = NOT a complete sentence ***Because*** introduces an adverb clause: ***because*** *+ subject + verb = an adverb clause*

MAIN CLAUSE   ADVERB CLAUSE
(d) He drank water *because* he was thirsty.
            (no comma)
 	
ADVERB CLAUSE   MAIN CLAUSE
(e) ***Because*** he was thirsty, he drank water.
            (comma)
	An adverb clause is connected to a main clause, as in (d) and (e).
	
	In (d): *main clause + no comma + adverb clause*
	
	In (e): *adverb clause + comma + main clause*
	
	Examples (d) and (e) have exactly the same meaning.

(f) *INCORRECT IN WRITING:* He drank water. *Because he was thirsty.*	Example (f) is incorrect in written English: ***Because he was thirsty*** cannot stand alone as a sentence that starts with a capital letter and ends with a period. It has to be connected to a main clause, as in (d) and (e).

(g) CORRECT IN SPEAKING:
      — Why did he drink some water?
      — **Because he was thirsty.**
	In spoken English, an adverb clause can be used as the short answer to a question, as in (g).

8-7 Connecting Ideas with *Even Though/Although*

(a) ***Even though*** *I was hungry,* I did not eat. I did not eat *even though* *I was hungry.*	***Even though*** and ***although*** introduce an adverb clause.
(b) ***Although*** *I was hungry,* I did not eat. I did not eat *although* *I was hungry.*	Examples (a) and (b) have the same meaning: *I was hungry, but I did not eat.*
COMPARE: (c) ***Because*** I was hungry, *I ate.* (d) ***Even though*** I was hungry, *I did not eat.*	***Because*** expresses an expected result, as in (c). ***Even though/although*** expresses an unexpected or opposite result, as in (d).

Chapter 9
Comparisons

9-1 Making Comparisons with *As . . . As*

(a) Tina is 21 years old. Sam is also 21. 　　Tina is *as old as* Sam (is). (b) Mike came *as quickly as* he could.	*As . . . as* is used to say that the two parts of a comparison are equal or the same in some way. 　　In (a): *as* + *adjective* + *as* 　　In (b): *as* + *adverb* + *as*
(c) Ted is 20. Tina is 21. 　　Ted is *not as old as* Tina. (d) Ted is *not quite as old as* Tina. (e) Amy is 5. She is *not nearly as old as* Tina.	Negative form: *not as . . . as.** *Quite* and *nearly* are often used with the negative. 　　In (d): *not quite as . . . as* = a small difference. 　　In (e): *not nearly as . . . as* = a big difference.
(f) Sam is *just as old as* Tina. (g) Ted is *nearly/almost as old as* Tina.	Common modifiers of *as . . . as* are *just* (meaning "exactly") and *nearly/almost.*

Tina 21	Sam 21	Ted 20	Amy 5

*Also possible: *not so . . . as: Ted is *not so old as* Tina.

9-2 Comparative and Superlative

(a) "A" is *older than* "B."	The comparative compares *this* to *that* or *these* to *those*.
(b) "A" and "B" are *older than* "C" and "D."	Form: ***-er*** or ***more*** (See Chart 9-3.)
(c) Ed is *more generous than* his brother.	Notice: A comparative is followed by ***than***.
(d) "A," "B," "C," and "D" are sisters. "A" is *the oldest* of *all* four sisters.	The superlative compares one part of a whole group to all the rest of the group.
(e) A woman in Turkey claims to be *the oldest person* in the world.	Form: ***-est*** or ***most*** (See Chart 9-3 for forms.)
(f) Ed is *the most generous person* in his family.	Notice: A superlative begins with ***the***.

A whale is *slower than* a shark.

9-3 Comparative and Superlative Forms of Adjectives and Adverbs

		Comparative	Superlative	
ONE-SYLLABLE ADJECTIVES	old wise	older wiser	the oldest the wisest	For most one-syllable adjectives, **-er** and **-est** are added.
TWO-SYLLABLE ADJECTIVES	famous pleasant	more famous more pleasant	the most famous the most pleasant	For most two-syllable adjectives, **more** and **most** are used.
	clever gentle friendly	cleverer more clever gentler more gentle friendlier more friendly	the cleverest the most clever the gentlest the most gentle the friendliest the most friendly	Some two-syllable adjectives use either **-er/-est** or **more/most**: *able, angry, clever, common, cruel, friendly, gentle, handsome, narrow, pleasant, polite, quiet, simple, sour.*
	busy pretty	busier prettier	the busiest the prettiest	**-Er** and **-est** are used with two-syllable adjectives that end in **-y**. The **-y** is changed to **-i**.
ADJECTIVES WITH THREE OR MORE SYLLABLES	important fascinating	more important more fascinating	the most important the most fascinating	**More** and **most** are used with long adjectives.
IRREGULAR ADJECTIVES	good bad	better worse	the best the worst	**Good** and **bad** have irregular comparative and superlative forms.
-*LY* ADVERBS	carefully slowly	more carefully more slowly	the most carefully the most slowly	**More** and **most** are used with adverbs that end in **-ly**.*
ONE-SYLLABLE ADVERBS	fast hard	faster harder	the fastest the hardest	The **-er** and **-est** forms are used with one-syllable adverbs.
IRREGULAR ADVERBS	well badly far	better worse farther/further	the best the worst the farthest/furthest	Both **farther** and **further** are used to compare physical distances: *I walked farther than my friend did.* OR *I walked further than my friend did.* **Further** also means "additional": *I need further information.* NOTE: **Farther** cannot be used when the meaning is "additional."

*Exception: **early** is both an adjective and an adverb. Forms: *earlier, earliest.*

9-4 Completing a Comparative

(a) I'm older *than **my brother*** (*is*). (b) I'm older *than he(is.)* (c) I'm older *than **him***. (*informal*)	In formal English, a subject pronoun (e.g., *he*) follows ***than***, as in (b). In everyday, informal spoken English, an object pronoun (e.g., *him*) often follows ***than***, as in (c).
(d) He works harder *than I **do***. (e) I arrived earlier *than they **did***.	Frequently an auxiliary verb follows the subject after ***than***. In (d): *than I do = than I work*
(f) *Ann's* hair is longer *than **Kate's***. (g) *Jack's* apartment is smaller *than **mine***.	A possessive noun (e.g., *Kate's*) or pronoun (e.g., *mine*) may follow ***than***.

9-5 Modifying Comparatives

(a) Tom is ***very*** old. (b) Ann drives ***very*** carefully.	***Very*** often modifies adjectives, as in (a), and adverbs, as in (b).
(c) INCORRECT: *Tom is very older than I am.* INCORRECT: *Ann drives very more carefully than she used to.*	***Very*** is NOT used to modify comparative adjectives and adverbs.
(d) Tom is ***much / a lot / far*** older than I am. (e) Ann drives ***much / a lot / far*** more carefully than she used to.	Instead, ***much***, ***a lot***, or ***far*** are used to modify comparative adjectives and adverbs, as in (d) and (e).
(f) Ben is ***a little*** (***bit***) older than I am OR (*informally*) me.	Another common modifier is ***a little/a little bit***, as in (f).

9-6 Comparisons with *Less ... Than* and *Not As ... As*

MORE THAN ONE SYLLABLE: (a) A pen is ***less*** expensive ***than*** a book. (b) A pen is ***not as*** expensive ***as*** a book.	The opposite of ***-er/more*** is expressed by ***less*** or ***not as ... as***. Examples (a) and (b) have the same meaning.
	Less and ***not as ... as*** are used with adjectives and adverbs of **more than one syllable**.
ONE SYLLABLE: (c) A pen is ***not as*** large ***as*** a book. INCORRECT: *A pen is less large than a book.*	Only ***not as ... as*** (NOT ***less***) is used with **one-syllable adjectives or adverbs**, as in (c).

9-7 Using *More* with Nouns

(a) Would you like some *more coffee*? (b) Not everyone is here. I expect *more people* to come later.	In (a): **Coffee** is a noun. When **more** is used with nouns, it often has the meaning of "additional." It is not necessary to use **than**.
(c) There are *more people* in China *than* there are in the United States.	**More** is also used with nouns to make complete comparisons by adding **than**.
(d) Do you have enough coffee, or would you like some *more*?	When the meaning is clear, the noun may be omitted and **more** can be used by itself.

9-8 Repeating a Comparative

(a) Because he was afraid, he walked *faster and faster*. (b) Life in the modern world is getting *more and more complicated*.	Repeating a comparative gives the idea that something becomes progressively greater, i.e., it increases in intensity, quality, or quantity.

9-9 Using Double Comparatives

(a) *The harder* you study, *the more* you will learn. (b) *The more* she studied, *the more* she learned. (c) *The warmer* the weather (is), *the better* I like it.	A double comparative has two parts; both parts begin with **the**, as in the examples. The second part of the comparison is the **result** of the first part. In (a): If you study harder, the result will be that you will learn more.

(d) — Should we ask Jenny and Jim to the party too?
    — Why not? *The more, the merrier.*
 	
 (e) — When should we leave?
    — *The sooner, the better.*
	The more, **the merrier** and **the sooner**, **the better** are two common expressions.
	
	 In (d): It is good to have more people at the party.
	
	 In (e): It is good if we leave as soon as we can.

9-10 Using Superlatives

(a) Tokyo is one of *the largest cities in the world.* (b) David is *the most generous person I have ever known.* (c) I have three books. These two are quite good, but this one is the *best* (book) *of all.*	Typical completions when a superlative is used: In (a): *superlative +* ***in*** *a place* (the world, this class, my family, the corporation, etc.) In (b): *superlative + adjective clause** In (c): *superlative +* ***of all***
(d) I took four final exams. The final in accounting was *the least difficult* of all.	***The least*** has the opposite meaning of ***the most***.
(e) Ali is *one of* the best *students* in this class. (f) *One of* the best *students* in this class *is* Ali.	Notice the pattern with ***one of***: ***one of*** *+ plural noun (+ singular verb)*
(g) I've *never* taken a *harder* test. (h) I've *never* taken a *hard* test.	***Never*** *+ comparative = superlative* Example (g) means "It was the hardest test I've ever taken." Compare (g) and (h).

*See Chapter 12 for more information about adjective clauses.

David

Paolo

Matt

Matt is *the youngest* of the three men.

9-11 Using *The Same, Similar, Different, Like, Alike*

(a) John and Mary have *the same books*. (b) John and Mary have *similar books*. (c) John and Mary have *different books*. (d) Their books are *the same*. (e) Their books are *similar*. (f) Their books are *different*.	*The same*, *similar*, and *different* are used as adjectives. Notice: *the* always precedes *same*.

(g) This book is *the same as* that one.
(h) This book is *similar to* that one.
(i) This book is *different from* that one.
	Notice: *the same* is followed by *as*;
	      similar is followed by *to*;
	      different is followed by *from*.*

(j) She is *the same age as* my mother. My shoes are *the same size as* yours.	A noun may come between *the same* and *as*, as in (j).

(k) My pen *is like* your pen.
(l) My pen *and* your pen *are alike*.
	Notice in (k) and (l):
	    noun + *be like* + *noun*
	    noun and noun + *be alike*

(m) She *looks like* her sister.
    It *looks like* rain.
    It *sounds like* thunder.
    This material *feels like* silk.
    That *smells like* gas.
    This chemical *tastes like* salt.
    Stop *acting like* a fool.
    He *seems like* a nice guy.
	In addition to following *be*, *like* also follows certain verbs, primarily those dealing with the senses.
	
	Notice the examples in (m).

(n) The twins *look alike*.
    We *think alike*.
    Most four-year-olds *act alike*.
    My sister and I *talk alike*.
    The little boys are *dressed alike*.
	Alike may follow a few verbs other than *be*.
	
	Notice the examples in (n).

*In informal speech, native speakers might use *than* instead of *from* after *different*. *From* is considered correct in formal English, unless the comparison is completed by a clause: *I have a different attitude now than I used to have.*

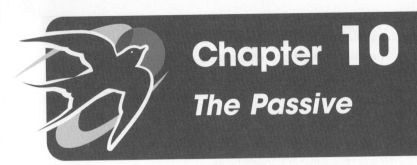

Chapter 10
The Passive

10-1 Active Sentences and Passive Sentences

Active (a) The mouse *ate* the cheese. **Passive** (b) The cheese *was eaten* by the mouse.	Examples (a) and (b) have the same meaning.

Active	**Passive**

Active 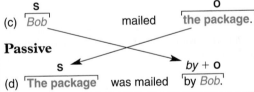 (c) *Bob* mailed **the package**. **Passive** (d) **The package** was mailed *by Bob*.	In (c): The object in an active sentence becomes the subject in a passive sentence. In (d): The subject in an active sentence is the object of *by* in a passive sentence.

10-2 Form of the Passive

	be +	**past participle**		Form of all passive verbs:
(a) Corn	*is*	*grown*	by farmers.	**be** + *past participle*
(b) Sara	*was*	*surprised*	by the news.	**Be** can be in any of its forms: *am, is, are, was, were,*
(c) The report	*will be*	*written*	by Mary.	*has been, have been, will be, etc.*

	Active	**Passive**
SIMPLE PRESENT	Farmers *grow* corn. ⟶	Corn *is grown* by farmers.
SIMPLE PAST	The news *surprised* Sara. ⟶	Sara *was surprised* by the news.
PRESENT PROGRESSIVE	Diana *is copying* the letters. ⟶	The letters *are being copied* by Diana.
PAST PROGRESSIVE	Diana *was copying* the letters. ⟶	The letters *were being copied* by Diana.
PRESENT PERFECT	Jack *has mailed* the letter. ⟶	The letter *has been mailed* by Jack.
FUTURE	Mr. Lee *will plan* the meeting. ⟶ Sue *is going to write* the report. ⟶	The meeting *will be planned* by Mr. Lee. The report *is going to be written* by Sue.

The truck *was damaged* by an old tree.

10-3 Transitive and Intransitive Verbs

Transitive

	S	V	O
(a)	Bob	*mailed*	*the letter.*
(b)	Mr. Lee	*signed*	*the check.*
(c)	A cat	*killed*	*the bird.*

A TRANSITIVE verb is a verb that is followed by an object. An object is a noun or a pronoun.

Intransitive

	S	V	
(d)	Something	*happened.*	
(e)	Kate	*came*	to our house.
(f)	The bird	*died.*	

An INTRANSITIVE verb is a verb that is NOT followed by an object.

Common Intransitive Verbs*

agree	die	happen	rise	stand
appear	exist	laugh	seem	stay
arrive	fall	live	sit	talk
become	flow	occur	sleep	wait
come	go	rain	sneeze	walk

Transitive Verbs

(g) ACTIVE: Bob *mailed* the letter.

(h) PASSIVE: The letter *was mailed* by Bob.

Only transitive verbs can be used in the passive.

Intransitive Verbs

(i) ACTIVE: Something *happened.*

(j) PASSIVE: (*not possible*)

(k) INCORRECT: Something *was happened.*

An intransitive verb is NOT used in the passive.

*To find out if a verb is transitive or intransitive, look in your dictionary. The usual abbreviations are v.t. (transitive) and v.i. (intransitive). Some verbs have both transitive and intransitive uses. For example:

transitive: *Students study books.*

intransitive: *Students study.*

Charles *was hypnotized* by a doctor.

10-4 Using the *by*-Phrase

(a) This sweater *was made* **by my aunt**.	The *by*-phrase is used in passive sentences when it is important to know who performs an action. In (a): **by my aunt** is important information.
(b) My sweater *was made* in Korea. (c) Spanish *is spoken* in Colombia. (d) That house *was built* in 1940. (e) Rice *is grown* in many countries.	Usually there is no *by*-phrase in a passive sentence. The passive is used when it is **not known or not important to know exactly who performs an action**. In (b): The exact person (or people) who made the sweater is not known and is not important to know, so there is no *by*-phrase in the passive sentence.
(f) **My aunt** is very skillful. **She** *made* this sweater. (g) A: I like your sweaters. B: Thanks. **This sweater** *was made by* my aunt. **That sweater** *was made by* my mother.	Usually the active is used when the speaker knows who performed the action, as in (f), where the focus of attention is on **my aunt**. In (g): Speaker B uses the passive WITH a *by*-phrase because he wants to focus attention on the subjects of the sentences. The focus of attention is on the two sweaters. The *by*-phrases add important information.

10-5 Passive Modal Auxiliaries

Active Modal Auxiliaries	Passive Modal Auxiliaries (*modal* + **be** + *past participle*)		Modal auxiliaries are often used in the passive.
Bob *will mail* it.	It	*will be mailed* by Bob.	FORM: *modal* + **be** + *past participle*
Bob *can mail* it.	It	*can be mailed* by Bob.	(See Chapter 7 for information about the meanings and uses of modal auxiliaries.)
Bob *should mail* it.	It	*should be mailed* by Bob.	
Bob *ought to mail* it.	It	*ought to be mailed* by Bob.	
Bob *must mail* it.	It	*must be mailed* by Bob.	
Bob *has to mail* it.	It	*has to be mailed* by Bob.	
Bob *may mail* it.	It	*may be mailed* by Bob.	
Bob *might mail* it.	It	*might be mailed* by Bob.	
Bob *could mail* it.	It	*could be mailed* by Bob.	

10-6 Using Past Participles as Adjectives (Non-Progressive Passive)

	be	+	adjective	
(a)	Paul	is	young.	
(b)	Paul	is	tall.	
(c)	Paul	is	hungry.	
	be	+	past participle	
(d)	Paul	is	married.	
(e)	Paul	is	tired.	
(f)	Paul	is	frightened.	

Be can be followed by an adjective, as in (a)–(c). The adjective describes or gives information about the subject of the sentence.

Be can be followed by a past participle (the passive form), as in (d)–(f). The past participle is often like an adjective. The past participle describes or gives information about the subject of the sentence. Past participles are used as adjectives in many common, everyday expressions.

(g) Paul *is married **to*** Susan.

(h) Paul *was excited **about*** the game.

(i) Paul *will be prepared **for*** the exam.

Often the past participles in these expressions are followed by particular prepositions + an object.
For example:

In (g): **married** is followed by **to** (+ *an object*)
In (h): **excited** is followed by **about** (+ *an object*)
In (i): **prepared** is followed by **for** (+ *an object*)

Some Common Expressions with *Be* + Past Participle

be acquainted (*with*)	be excited (*about*)	be opposed (*to*)
be bored (*with, by*)	be exhausted (*from*)	be pleased (*with*)
be broken	be finished (*with*)	be prepared (*for*)
be closed	be frightened (*of, by, about*)	be qualified (*for*)
be composed of	be gone (*from*)	be related (*to*)
be crowded (*with*)	be hurt	be satisfied (*with*)
be devoted (*to*)	be interested (*in*)	be scared (*of, by*)
be disappointed (*in, with*)	be involved (*in, with*)	be shut
be divorced (*from*)	be located in / south of / etc.	be spoiled
be done (*with*)	be lost	be terrified (*of, by*)
be drunk (*on*)	be made of	be tired (*of, from*)*
be engaged (*to*)	be married (*to*)	be worried (*about*)

*I'm **tired *of*** the cold weather. = *I've had enough cold weather. I want the weather to get warm.*
I'm **tired *from*** working hard all day. = *I'm tired because I worked hard all day.*

10-7 Participial Adjectives: *-ed* vs. *-ing*

Art **interests** me. (a) I am *interested* in art. INCORRECT: *I am interesting in art.* (b) Art is *interesting*. INCORRECT: *Art is interested.* The news **surprised** Kate. (c) Kate was *surprised*. (d) The news was *surprising*.	The past participle (**-ed**)* and the present participle (**-ing**) can be used as adjectives. In (a): The past participle (*interested*) describes how a person feels. In (b): The present participle (*interesting*) describes the **cause** of the feeling. The cause of the interest is art. In (c): *surprised* describes how Kate felt. The past participle carries a passive meaning: *Kate was surprised* **by the news**. In (d): **the news** was the cause of the surprise.
(e) Did you hear the *surprising news*? (f) Roberto fixed the *broken window*.	Like other adjectives, participial adjectives may follow **be**, as in examples (a) through (d), or they may come in front of nouns, as in (e) and (f).

*The past participle of regular verbs ends in **-ed**. For verbs that have irregular forms, see the inside front and back covers.

10-8 *Get* + Adjective; *Get* + Past Participle

***Get* + Adjective** (a) I *am getting hungry*. Let's eat. (b) Eric *got nervous* before the job interview.	**Get** can be followed by an adjective. **Get** gives the idea of change — the idea of becoming, beginning to be, growing to be. In (a): ***I'm getting hungry**.* = I wasn't hungry before, but now I'm beginning to be hungry.
***Get* + Past Participle** (c) I*'m getting tired*. Let's stop working. (d) Steve and Rita *got married* last month.	Sometimes **get** is followed by a past participle. The past participle after **get** is like an adjective; it describes the subject of the sentence.

Get + Adjective			**Get + Past Participle**		
get angry	get dry	get quiet	get acquainted	get drunk	get involved
get bald	get fat	get rich	get arrested	get engaged	get killed
get big	get full	get serious	get bored	get excited	get lost
get busy	get hot	get sick	get confused	get finished	get married
get close	get hungry	get sleepy	get crowded	get frightened	get scared
get cold	get interested	get thirsty	get divorced	get hurt	get sunburned
get dark	get late	get well	get done	get interested	get tired
get dirty	get nervous	get wet	get dressed	get invited	get worried
get dizzy	get old				

10-9 Using *Be Used/Accustomed To* and *Get Used/Accustomed To*

(a) I *am used to* hot weather. (b) I *am accustomed to* hot weather.	Examples (a) and (b) have the same meaning: "Living in a hot climate is usual and normal for me. I'm familiar with what it is like to live in a hot climate. Hot weather isn't strange or different to me."
(c) I *am used to living* in a hot climate. (d) I *am accustomed to living* in a hot climate.	Notice in (c) and (d): *to* (a preposition) is followed by the *-ing* form of a verb (a gerund).
(e) I just moved from Florida to Alaska. I have never lived in a cold climate before, but I *am getting used to* (*accustomed to*) the cold weather here.	In (e): *I'm getting used to/accustomed to* = something is beginning to seem usual and normal to me.

10-10 *Used To* vs. *Be Used To*

(a) I *used to live* in Chicago, but now I live in Tokyo. INCORRECT: *I used to living in Chicago.* INCORRECT: *I am used to live in a big city.*	In (a): *Used to* expresses the habitual past (see Chart 2-8, p. 14). It is followed by the **simple form of a verb.**
(b) I *am used to living* in a big city.	In (b): *be used to* is followed by the *-ing* **form of a verb** (a gerund).*

*NOTE: In both *used to* (habitual past) and *be used to,* the "d" is not pronounced.

10-11 Using *Be Supposed To*

(a) Mike *is supposed to call* me tomorrow. (IDEA: I expect Mike to call me tomorrow.) (b) We *are supposed to write* a composition. (IDEA: The teacher expects us to write a composition.)	*Be supposed to* is used to talk about an activity or event that is expected to occur. In (a): The idea of *is supposed to* is that Mike is expected (by me) to call me. I asked him to call me. He promised to call me. I expect him to call me.
(c) Alice *was supposed to be* home at ten, but she didn't get in until midnight. (IDEA: Someone expected Alice to be home at ten.)	In the past form, *be supposed to* often expresses the idea that an expected event did not occur, as in (c).

Chapter 11

Count/Noncount Nouns and Articles

11-1 *A* vs. *An*

(a) I have *a pencil*. (b) I live in *an apartment*. (c) I have *a small apartment*. (d) I live in *an old building*.	*A* and *an* are used in front of a singular noun (e.g., *pencil, apartment*). They mean "one." If a singular noun is modified by an adjective (e.g., *small, old*), *a* or *an* comes in front of the adjective, as in (c) and (d). *A* is used in front of words that begin with a consonant (*b, c, d, f, g*, etc.): *a boy, a bad day, a cat, a cute baby*. *An* is used in front of words that begin with the vowels *a, e, i*, and *o*: *an apartment, an angry man, an elephant, an empty room*, etc.
(e) I have *an umbrella*. (f) I saw *an ugly picture*. (g) I attend *a university*. (h) I had *a unique experience*.	For words that begin with the letter *u*: (1) *An* is used if the *u* is a vowel sound, as in *an umbrella, an uncle, an unusual day*. (2) *A* is used if the *u* is a consonant sound, as in *a university, a unit, a usual event*.
(i) He will arrive in *an hour*. (j) New Year's Day is *a holiday*.	For words that begin with the letter *h*: (1) *An* is used if the *h* is silent: *an hour, an honor, an honest person*. (2) *A* is used if the *h* is pronounced: *a holiday, a hotel, a high grade*.

A flamingo turns pink when it eats a lot of shrimp.

11-2 Count and Noncount Nouns

	Singular	Plural	
COUNT NOUN	*a* chair *one* chair	Ø chairs *two* chairs *some* chairs	A count noun: (1) can be counted with numbers: *one chair, two chairs, ten chairs, etc.* (2) can be preceded by **a/an** in the singular: *a chair.* (3) has a plural form ending in **-s** or **-es**: *chairs.**

NONCOUNT NOUN	Ø furniture
	 some furniture
		Ø
		 Ø
			A noncount noun:
			 (1) cannot be counted with numbers.
			     INCORRECT: *one furniture*
			 (2) is NOT immediately preceded by **a/an**.
			     INCORRECT: *a furniture*
			 (3) does NOT have a plural form (no final **-s**).
			     INCORRECT: *furnitures*

*See Chart 1-5, p. 4, and Chart 6-1, p. 38, for the spelling and pronunciation of **-s/-es**.

    a chicken   *some* chicken   *some* chicken**s**

11-3 Noncount Nouns

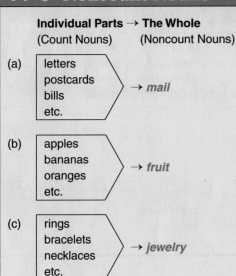

Individual Parts → The Whole
(Count Nouns)   (Noncount Nouns)

(a)
letters
postcards
bills
etc.
→ *mail*

(b)
apples
bananas
oranges
etc.
→ *fruit*

(c)
rings
bracelets
necklaces
etc.
→ *jewelry*

Noncount nouns usually refer to a whole group of things that is made up of many individual parts, a whole category made of different varieties.

For example, *furniture* is a noncount noun; it describes a whole category of things: *chairs, tables, beds, etc.*

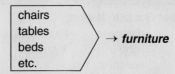

chairs
tables
beds
etc.
→ **furniture**

Mail, fruit, and *jewelry* are other examples of noncount nouns that refer to a whole category made up of individual parts.

Some Common Noncount Nouns: Whole Groups Made up of Individual Parts

A. clothing
   equipment
   food
   fruit
   furniture
   jewelry
   mail
   money
   scenery
   stuff
   traffic

B. homework
   housework
   work

C. advice
   information

D. history
   literature
   music
   poetry

E. grammar
   slang
   vocabulary

F. Arabic
   Chinese
   English
   German
   Indonesian
   Spanish
   Etc.

G. corn
   dirt
   flour
   hair
   pepper
   rice
   salt
   sand
   sugar

11-4 More Noncount Nouns

(a) **Liquids**		**Solids and Semi-Solids**				**Gases**
coffee	soup	bread	meat	chalk	paper	air
milk	tea	butter	beef	glass	soap	pollution
oil	water	cheese	chicken	gold	toothpaste	smog
		ice	fish	iron	wood	smoke

(b) **Things That Occur in Nature**						
weather	darkness	thunder				
rain	light	lightning				
snow	sunshine					

(c) **Abstractions***						
beauty	fun	health	ignorance	luck	selfishness	
courage	generosity	help	kindness	patience	time	
experience	happiness	honesty	knowledge	progress	violence	

*An abstraction is an idea. It has no physical form. A person cannot touch it.

11-5 Using *Several, A Lot Of, Many/Much,* and *A Few/A Little*

	Count	Noncount	
(a)	*several* chairs	Ø	**Several** is used only with count nouns.
(b)	*a lot of* chairs	*a lot of* furniture	**A lot of** is used with both count and noncount nouns.
(c)	*many* chairs	*much* furniture	**Many** is used with count nouns. **Much** is used with noncount nouns.
(d)	*a few* chairs	*a little* furniture	**A few** is used with count nouns. **A little** is used with noncount nouns.

11-6 Nouns That Can Be Count or Noncount

Quite a few nouns can be used as either count or noncount nouns. Examples of both count and noncount usages for some common nouns follow.

Noun	Used as a Noncount Noun	Used as a Count Noun
glass	(a) Windows are made of *glass*.	(b) I drank *a glass* of water. (c) Janet wears *glasses* when she reads.
hair	(d) Rita has brown *hair*.	(e) There's *a hair* on my jacket.
iron	(f) *Iron* is a metal.	(g) I pressed my shirt with *an iron*.
light	(h) I opened the curtain to let in *some light*.	(i) Please turn off *the lights* (*lamps*).
paper	(j) I need *some paper* to write a note.	(k) I wrote *a paper* for Professor Lee. (l) I bought *a paper* (*a newspaper*).
time	(m) How *much time* do you need to finish your work?	(n) How *many times* have you been to Mexico?
work	(o) I have *some work* to do tonight.	(p) That painting is *a work* of art.
coffee	(q) I had *some coffee* after dinner.	(r) *Two coffees*, please.
chicken/fish	(s) I ate *some chicken/some fish*.	(t) She drew a picture of *a chicken/a fish*.
experience	(u) I haven't had *much experience* with computers. (I don't have much knowledge or skill in using computers.)	(v) I had *many* interesting *experiences* on my trip. (Many interesting events happened to me on my trip.)

11-7 Using Units of Measure with Noncount Nouns

(a) I had some tea.
(b) I had *two cups of tea*.

(c) I ate some toast.
(d) I ate *one piece of toast*.

To mention a specific quantity of a noncount noun, speakers use units of measure such as *two cups of* or *one piece of*.

A unit of measure usually describes **the container** (*a cup of, a bowl of*), **the amount** (*a pound of, a quart of*),* or **the shape** (*a bar of soap, a sheet of paper*).

*Weight measure: *one pound* = 0.45 kilograms/kilos.
Liquid measure: *one quart* = 0.95 litres/liters; four quarts = one gallon = 3.8 litres/liters.

11-8 Guidelines for Article Usage

TO MAKE A GENERALIZATION

Singular Count Nouns: *A/An*

(a) *A dog* makes a good pet. (b) *An apple* is red. (c) *A pencil* contains lead.	In (a): The speaker is talking about any dog, all dogs, dogs in general.

Plural Count Nouns: Ø

(d) Ø *Dogs* make good pets. (e) Ø *Apples* are red. (f) Ø *Pencils* contain lead.	In (d): The speaker is talking about any dog, all dogs, dogs in general. NOTE: Examples (a) and (d) have the same meaning.

Noncount Nouns: Ø

(g) Ø *Fruit* is good for you. (h) Ø *Coffee* contains caffeine. (i) I like Ø *music*.	In (g): The speaker is talking about any fruit, all fruit, fruit in general.

TO TALK ABOUT NON-SPECIFIC PERSON(S) OR THING(S)

Singular Count Nouns: *A/An*

(j) I saw *a dog* in my yard. (k) Mary ate *an apple*. (l) I need *a pencil*.	In (j): The speaker is saying, "I saw one dog (not two dogs, some dogs, many dogs). It wasn't a specific dog (e.g., your dog, the neighbor's dog, that dog). It was only one dog out of the whole group of animals called dogs."

Plural Count Nouns: *Some*

(m) I saw *some dogs* in my yard. (n) Mary bought *some apples*. (o) Bob has *some pencils* in his pocket.	In (m): The speaker is saying, "I saw more than one dog. They weren't specific dogs (e.g., your dogs, the neighbor's dogs, those dogs). The exact number of dogs isn't important (two dogs, five dogs); I'm simply saying that I saw an indefinite number of dogs." See Chart 11-5 for other words that can be used with plural count nouns, such as *several, a few*, and *a lot of*.

Noncount Nouns: *Some*

(p) I bought *some fruit*. (q) Bob drank *some coffee*. (r) Would you like to listen to *some music*?	In (p): The speaker is saying, "I bought an indefinite amount of fruit. The exact amount (e.g., two pounds of fruit, four bananas, and two apples) isn't important. And I'm not talking about specific fruit (e.g., that fruit, the fruit in that bowl.)" See Chart 11-5 for other words that can be used with noncount nouns, such as *a little* and *a lot of*.

11-8 Guidelines for Article Usage (*continued*)

THE SPEAKER AND THE LISTENER ARE THINKING ABOUT THE SAME SPECIFIC PERSON(S) OR THINGS.

Singular Count Nouns: *The*

(s) Did you feed *the* dog? (t) Kay is in *the kitchen*. (u) *The sun* is shining. (v) Please close *the* door. (w) *The president* is speaking on TV tonight.	In (s): The speaker and the listener are thinking about the same specific dog. The listener knows which dog the speaker is talking about: the dog that they own, the dog that they feed every day. There is only one dog that the speaker could possibly be talking about.

(x) I had a banana and an apple. I gave *the* banana to Mary.	In (x): A speaker uses *the* when she/he mentions a noun the second time.
	      First mention: *I had **a** banana* . . .
	      Second mention: *I gave **the** banana* . . .
	
	 In the second mention, the listener now knows which banana the speaker is talking about: the banana the speaker had (not the banana John had, not the banana in that bowl).

Plural Count Nouns: *The*

(y) Did you feed *the* dogs? (z) *The pencils* on that desk are Jim's. (aa) Please turn off *the lights*.	In (y): The speaker and the listener are thinking about more than one dog, and they are thinking about the same specific dogs.
(bb) I had some bananas and apples. I gave *the* bananas to Mary.	In (bb) *the* is used for second mention.

Noncount Nouns: *The*

(cc) *The fruit* in this bowl is ripe. (dd) I can't hear you. *The music* is too loud. (ee) *The air* smells fresh today.	When *the* is used with noncount nouns, the speaker knows or can assume the listener is familiar with and thinking about the same specific thing.
(ff) I drank some coffee and some milk. *The coffee* was hot.	In (ff): *the* is used for second mention. NOTE: *a*, *an*, and Ø are not possible for the situations described in (s) through (ff).

11-9 Using *The* or Ø with Names

(a) We met Ø *Mr. Wang.* I know Ø *Doctor Smith.* Ø *President Rice* has been in the news.	**The** is NOT used with titled names. INCORRECT: *We met the Mr. Wang.*
(b) He lives in Ø *Europe.* Ø *Asia* is the largest continent. Have you ever been to Ø *Africa?*	**The** is NOT used with the names of continents. INCORRECT: *He lives in the Europe.*
(c) He lives in Ø *France.* Ø *Brazil* is a large country. Have you ever been to Ø *Thailand?* (d) He lives in **the United States.** **The Netherlands** is in Europe. Have you ever been to **the Philippines?**	**The** is NOT used with the names of most countries. INCORRECT: *He lives in the France.* **The** is used in the names of only a few countries, as in (d). Others: *the Czech Republic, the United Arab Emirates, the Dominican Republic.*
(e) He lives in Ø *Paris.* Ø *New York* is the largest city in the United States. Have you ever been to Ø *Istanbul?*	**The** is NOT used with the names of cities. INCORRECT: *He lives in the Paris.*
(f) **The Nile River** is long. They crossed **the Pacific Ocean.** **The Yellow Sea** is in Asia. (g) Chicago is on Ø *Lake Michigan.* Ø *Lake Titicaca* lies on the border between Peru and Bolivia.	**The** is used with the names of rivers, oceans, and seas. **The** is NOT used with the names of lakes.
(h) We hiked in **the Alps.** **The Andes** are in South America. (i) He climbed Ø *Mount Everest.* Ø *Mount Fuji* is in Japan.	**The** is used with the names of mountain ranges. **The** is NOT used with the names of individual mountains.

Teal likes to hike in *Italy*.

11-10 Capitalization

Capitalize

1. The first word of a sentence	We saw a movie last night. It was very good.	*Capitalize* = use a big letter, not a small letter
2. The names of people	I met George Adams yesterday.	
3. Titles used with the names of people	I saw Doctor (Dr.) Smith. There's Professor (Prof.) Lee.	I saw a doctor. BUT I saw Doctor Wilson.
4. Months, days, holidays	I was born in April. Bob arrived last Monday. It snowed on New Year's Day.	NOTE: Seasons are not capitalized: *spring, summer, fall/autumn, winter.*
5. The names of places: city state/province country continent	He lives in Chicago. She was born in California. They are from Mexico. Tibet is in Asia.	She lives in a city. BUT She lives in New York City.
ocean lake river desert mountain	They crossed the Atlantic Ocean. Chicago is on Lake Michigan. The Nile River flows north. The Sahara Desert is in Africa. We visited the Rocky Mountains.	They crossed a river. They crossed the Yellow River.
school business	I go to the University of Florida. I work for the Boeing Company.	I go to a university. BUT I go to the University of Texas.
street building park, zoo	He lives on Grand Avenue. We have class in Ritter Hall. I went jogging in Forest Park.	We went to a park. BUT We went to Central Park.
6. The names of courses	I'm taking Chemistry 101.	Here's your history book. BUT I'm taking History 101.
7. The titles of books, articles, movies	*Gone with the Wind* *The Sound of the Mountain*	Capitalize the first word of a title. Capitalize all other words except articles (*the, a/an*), coordinating conjunctions (*and, but, or*), and short prepositions (*with, in, at, etc.*).
8. The names of languages and nationalities	She speaks Spanish. We discussed Japanese customs.	Words that refer to the names of languages and nationalities are always capitalized.
9. The names of religions	Buddhism, Christianity, Hinduism, Islam, and Judaism are major religions in the world. Talal is a Muslim.	Words that refer to the names of religions are always capitalized.

Chapter 12
Adjective Clauses

12-1 Adjective Clauses: Introduction

Adjectives	Adjective Clauses
An **adjective** modifies a noun. *Modify* means to change a little. An adjective describes or gives information about the noun. (See Chart 6-8, p. 160.)	An **adjective clause*** modifies a noun. It describes or gives information about a noun.
An adjective usually comes in front of a noun.	An adjective clause follows a noun.
adjective + noun (a) I met a ⌐*kind*¬ ⌐*man*.¬ adjective + noun (b) I met a ⌐*famous*¬ ⌐*man*.¬	noun + adjective clause (c) I met a ⌐*man*¬ ⌐*who is kind to everybody*.¬ noun + adjective clause (d) I met a ⌐*man*¬ ⌐*who is a famous poet*.¬ noun + adjective clause (e) I met a ⌐*man*¬ ⌐*who lives in Chicago*.¬

*GRAMMAR TERMINOLOGY (1) *I met a man* = an independent clause; it is a complete sentence. (2) *He lives in Chicago* = an independent clause; it is a complete sentence. (3) *who lives in Chicago* = a dependent clause; it is NOT a complete sentence. (4) *I met a man who lives in Chicago* = an independent clause + a dependent clause; a complete sentence.	A **clause** is a structure that has a subject and a verb. There are two kinds of clauses: **independent** and **dependent**. • An **independent clause** is a main clause and can stand alone as a sentence, as in (1) and (2). • A **dependent clause**, as in (3), cannot stand alone as a sentence. It must be connected to an independent clause, as in (4).

12-2 Using *Who* and *That* in Adjective Clauses to Describe People

(a) The man is friendly.	**S V** *He* lives next to me. ↓ *who* ↓ **S V** *who* lives next to me	In adjective clauses, **who** and **that** are used as subject pronouns to describe people. In (a): **He** is a subject pronoun. **He** refers to "the man." To make an adjective clause, change **he** to **who**. **Who** is a subject pronoun. **Who** refers to "the man."
(b) The man **who** *lives next to me* is friendly.		
(c) The woman is talkative.	**S V** *She* lives next to me. ↓ *that* ↓ **S V** *that* lives next to me	**That** is also a subject pronoun and can replace **who**, as in (d). The subject pronouns **who** and **that** cannot be omitted from an adjective clause. INCORRECT: *The woman lives next to me is talkative.* As subject pronouns, both **who** and **that** are common in conversation, but **who** is more common in writing.
(d) The woman **that** *lives next to me* is talkative.		In (b) and (d): The adjective clause immediately follows the noun it modifies. INCORRECT: *The woman is talkative that lives next to me.*

The man **who** *is giving this party* is actually very shy.

12-3 Using Object Pronouns in Adjective Clauses to Describe People

(a) The man was friendly.	**S V O** I met *him*. ↓ *that*	In adjective clauses, pronouns are used as the object of a verb to describe people. In (a): *him* is an object pronoun. *Him* refers to "the man." One way to make an adjective clause is to change *him* to *that*. *That* is the object pronoun. *That* refers to "the man." *That* comes at the beginning of an adjective clause. An object pronoun can be omitted from an adjective clause, as in (c).
O S V (b) The man *that* *I met* was friendly. (c) The man Ø *I met* was friendly.		
(d) The man was friendly. I met	**S V O** *him*. ↓ *who* *whom*	*Him* can also be changed to *who* or *whom*, as in (e) and (f). As an object pronoun, *that* is more common than *who* in speaking. Ø is the most common choice for both speaking and writing. *Whom* is generally used only in very formal writing.
O S V (e) The man *who* *I met* was friendly. (f) The man *whom* *I met* was friendly.		

The **girl** *who was sitting next to me on the roller coaster* was laughing.

12-4 Using Pronouns in Adjective Clauses to Describe Things

(a) The river is polluted. **S** **V** *It* ↓ *that* *which* flows through the town.	**Who** and **whom** refer to people. **Which** refers to things. **That** can refer to either people or things.
S **V** (b) The river **that** *flows through the town* is polluted. (c) The river **which** *flows through the town* is polluted.	In (a): To make an adjective clause, change **it** to **that** or **which**. **It**, **that**, and **which** all refer to a thing (the river). (b) and (c) have the same meaning, but (b) is more common than (c) in speaking and writing.
	When **that** and **which** are used as the subject of an adjective clause, they CANNOT be omitted. *INCORRECT:* The river flows through the town is polluted.
S **V** **O** (d) The books were expensive. I bought **them**. ↓ **that** **which**	**That** or **which** can be used as an object in an adjective clause, as in (e) and (f). An object pronoun can be omitted from an adjective clause, as in (g).
O **S** **V** (e) The books **that** *I bought* were expensive. (f) The books **which** *I bought* were expensive. (g) The books Ø *I bought* were expensive.	(e), (f), and (g) have the same meaning. In speaking, **that** and Ø are more common than **which**. In writing, **that** is the most common, and Ø is rare.

12-5 Singular and Plural Verbs in Adjective Clauses

(a) I know the **man** *who **is** sitting over there.*	In (a): The verb in the adjective clause (**is**) is singular because **who** refers to a singular noun, **man**.
(b) I know the **people** *who **are** sitting over there.*	In (b): The verb in the adjective clause (**are**) is plural because **who** refers to a plural noun, **people**.

12-6 Using Prepositions in Adjective Clauses

		PREP	**OBJ**		
(a)	The man was nice. I talked	*to*	*him.*		

		OBJ		**PREP**	
(b)	The man	*that*	*I talked*	*to*	was nice.
(c)	The man	*Ø*	*I talked*	*to*	was nice.
(d)	The man	*whom*	*I talked*	*to*	was nice.
		PREP	**OBJ**		
(e)	The man	*to*	*whom*	*I talked*	was nice.

			PREP	**OBJ**	
(f)	The chair is hard. I am sitting		*in*	*it.*	

		OBJ		**PREP**	
(g)	The chair	*that*	*I am sitting*	*in*	is hard.
(h)	The chair	*Ø*	*I am sitting*	*in*	is hard.
(i)	The chair	*which*	*I am sitting*	*in*	is hard.
		PREP	**OBJ**		
(j)	The chair	*in*	*which*	*I am sitting*	is hard.

That, whom, and ***which*** can be used as the object (OBJ) of a preposition (PREP) in an adjective clause.

REMINDER: An object pronoun can be omitted from an adjective clause, as in (c) and (h).

In very formal English, a preposition comes at the beginning of an adjective clause, followed by either ***whom*** or ***which***, as in (e) and (j). This is not common in spoken English.

NOTE: In (e) and (j), ***that*** or ***who*** cannot be used, and the pronoun CANNOT be omitted.

(b), (c), (d), and (e) have the same meaning.

(g), (h), (i), and (j) have the same meaning.

12-7 Using *Whose* in Adjective Clauses

(a)	The man called the police. *His car* → *whose car* was stolen.	***Whose**** shows possession. In (a): *His car* can be changed to *whose car* to make an adjective clause. In (b): *whose car was stolen* = an adjective clause.
(b)	The man ***whose car*** *was stolen* called the police.	
(c)	I know a girl. *Her brother* → *whose brother* is a movie star.	In (c): *Her brother* can be changed to *whose brother* to make an adjective clause.
(d)	I know a girl ***whose brother*** *is a movie star.*	
(e)	The people were friendly. We bought *their house.* → *whose house*	In (e): *Their house* can be changed to *whose house* to make an adjective clause.
(f)	The people ***whose house*** *we bought* were friendly.	

*****Whose*** and ***who's*** have the same pronunciation but NOT the same meaning.
Who's = ***who is:*** *Who's (Who is) your teacher?*

Chapter 13
Gerunds and Infinitives

13-1 Verb + Gerund

VERB GERUND (a) I *enjoy walking* in the park.	A gerund is the *-ing* form of a verb. It is used as a noun. In (a): *walking* is a gerund. It is used as the object of the verb *enjoy*.

Common Verbs Followed by Gerunds
enjoy   (b) I *enjoy working* in my garden.
finish   (c) Ann *finished studying* at midnight.
quit   (d) David *quit smoking*.
mind   (e) Would you *mind opening* the window?
postpone   (f) I *postponed doing* my homework.
put off   (g) I *put off doing* my homework.
keep (on)   (h) *Keep* (*on*) *working*. Don't stop.
consider   (i) I'm *considering going* to Hawaii.
think about   (j) I'm *thinking about going* to Hawaii.
discuss   (k) They *discussed getting* a new car.
talk about   (l) They *talked about getting* a new car.
	The verbs in the list are followed by gerunds. The list also contains phrasal verbs (e.g., *put off*) that are followed by gerunds.
	
	The verbs in the list are NOT followed by *to* + the simple form of a verb (an infinitive).
	   INCORRECT: I enjoy to walk in the park.
	   INCORRECT: Bob finished to study.
	   INCORRECT: I'm thinking to go to Hawaii.
	
	See Chart 2-2, p. 8, for the spelling of *-ing* verb forms.

(m) I *considered not going* to class.	Negative form: *not* + gerund

13-2 Go + -ing

(a) *Did* you *go shopping* yesterday? (b) I *went swimming* last week. (c) Bob *hasn't gone fishing* in years.	*Go* is followed by a gerund in certain idiomatic expressions about activities. NOTE: There is no *to* between *go* and the gerund. *INCORRECT: Did you go to shopping?*

Common Expressions with *go* + *-ing*

go boating	go dancing	go jogging	go (window) shopping	go (water) skiing
go bowling	go fishing	go running	go sightseeing	go skydiving
go camping	go hiking	go sailing	go (ice) skating	go swimming

13-3 Verb + Infinitive

(a) Tom *offered to lend* me some money.	Some verbs are followed by an infinitive.
(b) I've *decided to buy* a new car.	Infinitive = *to* + *the simple form of a verb*
(c) I've *decided not to keep* my old car.	Negative form: *not* + *infinitive*

Common Verbs Followed by Infinitives

want	hope	decide	seem	learn (how)
need	expect	promise	appear	try
would like	plan	offer	pretend	
would love	intend	agree		(can't) afford
	mean	refuse		(can't) wait

13-4 Verb + Gerund or Infinitive

(a) It *began raining*.	Some verbs are followed by either a gerund, as in (a), or an infinitive, as in (b). Usually there is no difference in meaning.
(b) It *began to rain*.	Examples (a) and (b) have the same meaning.

Common Verbs Followed by Either a Gerund or an Infinitive

begin	like*	hate
start	love*	can't stand
continue		

*COMPARE: *Like* and *love* can be followed by either a gerund or an infinitive:
  I like going / to go to movies. I love playing / to play chess.
Would like and *would love* are followed by infinitives:
  I would like *to go* to a movie tonight. I'd love *to play* a game of chess right now.

13-5 Preposition + Gerund

(a) Kate *insisted **on coming*** with us. (b) We're *excited **about going*** to Tahiti. (c) I *apologized **for being*** late.	A preposition is followed by a gerund, not an infinitive. In (a): The preposition (*on*) is followed by a gerund (*coming*).

Common Expressions with Prepositions Followed by Gerunds

be afraid **of** (doing something) apologize **for** believe **in** dream **about/of** be excited **about** feel **like** forgive (someone) **for**	be good **at** insist **on** instead **of** be interested **in** look forward **to** be nervous **about** plan **on**	be responsible **for** stop (someone) **from** thank (someone) **for** be tired **of** worry **about**/be worried **about**

13-6 Using *By* and *With* to Express How Something Is Done

(a) Pat turned off the TV *by pushing* the "off" button.	***By** + a gerund* is used to express how something is done.
(b) Mary goes to work *by bus*. (c) Andrea stirred her coffee *with a spoon*.	***By*** or ***with*** followed by a noun is also used to express how something is done.

BY IS USED FOR MEANS OF TRANSPORTATION AND COMMUNICATION

by (air)plane by boat by bus by car	by subway* by taxi by train by foot (*or:* on foot)	by mail/email by (tele)phone by fax (*but:* in person)	by air by land by sea

OTHER USES OF *BY*

by chance by choice	by mistake by hand**	by check (*but:* in cash) by credit card

WITH IS USED FOR INSTRUMENTS OR PARTS OF THE BODY

I cut down the tree *with an ax* (by using an ax).
I swept the floor *with a broom*.
She pointed to a spot on the map *with her finger*.

* *by subway* = American English; *by underground, by tube* = British English.

** The expression ***by hand*** is usually used to mean that something was made by a person, not by a machine: *This rug was made **by hand**.* (A person, not a machine, made this rug.)
   COMPARE: *I touched his shoulder **with my hand**.*

13-7 Using Gerunds as Subjects; Using *It* + Infinitive

(a) *Riding* horses is fun.	Examples (a) and (b) have the same meaning.
(b) *It* is fun *to ride* horses.	In (a): A gerund (*riding*) is the subject of the sentence.
	Notice: The verb (*is*) is singular because a gerund is singular.*
(c) *Coming* to class on time is important.	In (b): *It* is used as the subject of the sentence. *It* has the same
(d) *It* is important *to come* to class on time.	meaning as the infinitive phrase at the end of the sentence: *it*
	means *to ride horses.*

*It is also correct (but less common) to use an infinitive as the subject of a sentence: *To ride horses is fun.*

13-8 *It* + Infinitive: Using *For (Someone)*

(a) *You* should study hard.	Examples (a) and (b) have a similar meaning.
(b) It is important *for you* to study hard.	Notice the pattern in (b):
(c) *Mary* should study hard.	*It is* + adjective + *for* (someone) + infinitive phrase
(d) It is important *for Mary* to study hard.	
(e) *We* don't have to go to the meeting.	
(f) It isn't necessary *for us* to go to the meeting.	
(g) *A dog* can't talk.	
(h) It is impossible *for a dog* to talk.	

13-9 Expressing Purpose with *In Order To* and *For*

—Why did you go to the post office?	**In order to** expresses purpose. It answers the question "Why?"
(a) I went to the post office *because I wanted to mail a letter.*	
(b) I went to the post office *in order to mail a letter.*	In (c): *in order* is frequently omitted. Examples
(c) I went to the post office *to mail* a letter.	(a), (b), and (c) have the same meaning.
(d) I went to the post office *for some stamps.*	**For** is also used to express purpose, but it is
(e) I went to the post office *to buy* some stamps.	a preposition and is followed by a noun
INCORRECT: *I went to the post office for to buy some stamps.*	phrase, as in (d).
INCORRECT: *I went to the post office for buying some stamps.*	

13-10 Using Infinitives with *Too* and *Enough*

too + adjective + (**for someone**) + infinitive	Infinitives often follow expressions with **too**. **Too** comes in front of an adjective. In the speaker's mind, the use of **too** implies a negative result.
(a) That box is **too** *heavy* **to** *lift*. (b) A piano is **too** *heavy* **for** *me* **to** *lift*. (c) That box is **too** *heavy* **for** *Bob* **to** *lift*.	
enough + noun + infinitive	COMPARE: *The box is too heavy. I can't lift it.* *The box is very heavy, but I can lift it.*
(d) I don't have **enough** *money* **to** *buy* that car. (e) Did you have **enough** *time* **to** *finish* the test?	
adjective + **enough** + infinitive	Infinitives often follow expressions with **enough**. **Enough** comes in front of a noun.* **Enough** follows an adjective.
(f) Jimmy isn't *old* **enough** **to** *go* to school. (g) Are you *hungry* **enough** **to** *eat* three sandwiches?	

*****Enough** can also follow a noun: *I don't have **money enough** to buy that car.* In everyday English, however, **enough** usually comes in front of a noun.

The piano is *too heavy* for Ed and Jim to move.

Chapter 14
Noun Clauses

14-1 Noun Clauses: Introduction

(a) I know **his address**. S V O (noun phrase) (b) I know **where he lives**. S V O (noun clause)	Verbs are often followed by objects. The object is usually a noun phrase.* In (a): **his address** is a noun phrase; **his address** is the object of the verb *know*. Some verbs can be followed by noun clauses.* In (b): **where he lives** is a noun clause; **where he lives** is the object of the verb *know*.
(c) I know *where **he lives**.* S V O S V	A noun clause has its own subject and verb. In (c): **he** is the subject of the noun clause; **lives** is the verb of the noun clause.
(d) I know **where my book is**. (noun clause)	A noun clause can begin with a question word. (See Chart 14-2.)
(e) I don't know **if Ed is married**. (noun clause)	A noun clause can begin with **if** or **whether**. (See Chart 14-3.)
(f) I know **that the world is round**. (noun clause)	A noun clause can begin with **that**. (See Chart 14-4.)

*A *phrase* is a group of related words. It does NOT contain a subject and a verb.

A *clause* is a group of related words. It contains a subject and a verb.

14-2 Noun Clauses That Begin with a Question Word

These question words can be used to introduce a noun clause: **when**, **where**, **why**, **how**, **who**, (**whom**), **what**, **which**, **whose**.

Information Question	Noun Clause	Notice in the examples: Usual question word order is NOT used in a noun clause.
Where *does he live?*	(a) I don't know *where* **he lives**. 　　　　　　　　S　V	*INCORRECT:* I know where does he live. *CORRECT:* I know where he lives.
When *did they leave?*	(b) Do you know *when* **they left**?* 　　　　　　　　S　V	
What *did she say?*	(c) Please tell me *what* **she said**. 　　　　　　　　S　V	
Why *is Tom* absent?	(d) I wonder *why* **Tom is** absent. 　　　　　　　S　V	
Who *is* *that boy?* 　V　S	(e) Tell me *who* *that boy* *is*. 　　　　　S　　　V	A noun or pronoun that follows main verb **be** in a question comes in front of **be** in a noun clause, as in (e) and (f).
Whose pen *is* *this?* 　　　V　S	(f) Do you know *whose pen* *this* *is?* 　　　　　　　　　S　　V	
Who *is* in the office? 　S　V	(g) I don't know *who* *is* in the office. 　　　　　　　S　　V	A prepositional phrase (e.g., *in the office*) does not come in front of **be** in a noun clause, as in (g) and (h).
Whose keys *are* on the counter? 　S　　　V	(h) I wonder *whose keys* *are* on the counter. 　　　　　　　S　　　　V	
Who *came* to class? 　S　V	(i) I don't know *who came* to class. 　　　　　　　S　V	In (i) and (j): Question word order and noun clause word order are the same when the question word is used as a subject.
What happened? 　S	(j) Tell me *what happened*. 　　　　S　V	

*A question mark is used at the end of this sentence because *Do you know* asks a question.
　Example: *Do you know when they left?*
Do you know asks a question; *when they left* is a noun clause.

14-3 Noun Clauses That Begin with *If* or *Whether*

Yes/No Question	Noun Clause	When a yes/no question is changed to a noun clause, *if* is usually used to introduce the clause.*
Is Eric at home?	(a) I don't know *if Eric is at home*.	
Does the bus stop here?	(b) Do you know *if the bus stops here*?	
Did Alice go to Chicago?	(c) I wonder *if Alice went to Chicago*.	

(d) I don't know *if Eric is at home **or not***.	When *if* introduces a noun clause, the expression ***or not*** sometimes comes at the end of the clause, as in (d).
(e) I don't know ***whether*** Eric is at home (*or not*).	In (e): ***whether*** has the same meaning as *if*.

*See Chart 14-10 for the use of *if* with ***ask*** in reported speech.

14-4 Noun Clauses That Begin with *That*

	A noun clause can be introduced by the word ***that.***
S V O (a) I think *that Mr. Jones is a good teacher.* (b) I hope *that you can come to the game.* (c) Mary realizes *that she should study harder.* (d) I dreamed *that I was on the top of a mountain.*	In (a): *that Mr. Jones is a good teacher* is a noun clause. It is the object of the verb ***think***. *That*-clauses are frequently used as the objects of verbs that express mental activity.
(e) I think *that Mr. Jones is a good teacher.* (f) I think Ø *Mr. Jones is a good teacher.*	The word ***that*** is often omitted, especially in speaking. Examples (e) and (f) have the same meaning.

Common Verbs Followed by *That*-clauses*

agree that	dream that	know that	realize that
assume that	feel that	learn that	remember that
believe that	forget that	notice that	say that
decide that	guess that	predict that	suppose that
discover that	hear that	prove that	think that
doubt that	hope that	read that	understand that

*See Appendix Chart A-4 for more verbs that can be followed by *that*-clauses.

14-5 Other Uses of *That*-Clauses

(a) I'm *sure that* the bus stops here. (b) I'm *glad that* you're feeling better today. (c) I'm *sorry that* I missed class yesterday. (d) I *was disappointed that* you couldn't come.	*That*-clauses can follow certain expressions with *be* + *adjective* or *be* + *past participle*. The word *that* can be omitted with no change in meaning: *I'm sure Ø the bus stops here.*
(e) *It is true that* the world is round. (f) *It is a fact that* the world is round.	Two common expressions followed by *that*-clauses are: *It is true (that)* . . . . *It is a fact (that)* . . . .

Common Expressions Followed by *That*-clauses*

be afraid that	be disappointed that	be sad that	be upset that
be angry that	be glad that	be shocked that	be worried that
be aware that	be happy that	be sorry that	
be certain that	be lucky that	be sure that	It is a fact that
be convinced that	be pleased that	be surprised that	It is true that

*See Appendix Chart A-5 for more expressions that can be followed by *that*-clauses.

14-6 Substituting *So* for a *That*-Clause in Conversational Responses

(a) A: Is Ana from Peru? B: **I think so.** (*so = that Ana is from Peru*)	***Think*, *believe*, and *hope*** are frequently followed by *so* in conversational English in response to a yes/no question. They are alternatives to *yes*, *no*, or *I don't know*. *So* replaces a *that*-clause. INCORRECT: *I think so that Ana is from Peru.*
(b) A: Does Judy live in Dallas? B: **I believe so.** (*so = that Judy lives in Dallas*)	
(c) A: Did you pass the test? B: **I hope so.** (*so = that I passed the test*)	
(d) A: Is Jack married? B: *I don't* think *so.* / I *don't* believe *so.*	Negative usage of **think so** and **believe so**: *do not think so / do not believe so*
(e) A: Did you fail the test? B: **I hope** *not.*	Negative usage of **hope** in conversational responses: *hope not.* In (e): **I hope not** = I hope I didn't fail the test. INCORRECT: *I don't hope so.*
(f) A: Do you want to come with us? B: Oh, I don't know. **I guess** *so.*	Other common conversational responses: *I guess so. I guess not.* *I suppose so. I suppose not.* NOTE: In spoken English, **suppose** often sounds like "spoze."

14-7 Quoted Speech

Sometimes we want to quote a speaker's words — to write a speaker's exact words. Exact quotations are used in many kinds of writing, such as newspaper articles, stories, novels, and academic papers. When we quote a speaker's words, we use quotation marks.

(a) **SPEAKERS' EXACT WORDS** Jane: Cats are fun to watch. Mike: Yes, I agree. They're graceful and playful. Do you have a cat?	(b) **QUOTING THE SPEAKERS' WORDS** Jane said, "Cats are fun to watch." Mike said, "Yes, I agree. They're graceful and playful. Do you have a cat?"

(c) **HOW TO WRITE QUOTATIONS**

1. Add a comma after *said*.* ———————————→ Jane said,
2. Add quotation marks.** ———————————→ Jane said, "
3. Capitalize the first word of the quotation. ———→ Jane said, "Cats
4. Write the quotation. Add a final period. ————→ Jane said, "Cats are fun to watch.
5. Add quotation marks **after** the period. ———→ Jane said, "Cats are fun to watch."

(d) Mike said, "Yes, I agree. They're graceful and playful. Do you have a cat?" (e) INCORRECT: *Mike said, "Yes, I agree." "They're graceful and playful." "Do you have a cat?"*	When there are two (or more) sentences in a quotation, put the quotation marks at the beginning and end of the whole quote, as in (d). Do NOT put quotation marks around each sentence. As with a period, put the quotation marks after a question mark at the end of a quote.
(f) "Cats are fun to watch," Jane said. (g) "Do you have a cat?" Mike asked.	In (f): Notice that a comma (not a period) is used at the end of the QUOTED SENTENCE because **Jane said** comes after the quote. In (g): Notice that a question mark (not a comma) is used at the end of the QUOTED QUESTION.

*Other common verbs besides *say* that introduce questions: *admit, announce, answer, ask, complain, explain, inquire, report, reply, shout, state, write.*

**Quotation marks are called "inverted commas" in British English.

14-8 Quoted Speech vs. Reported Speech

QUOTED SPEECH (a) Ann said, "*I'm* hungry." (b) Tom said, "*I need my* pen."	QUOTED SPEECH = giving a speaker's exact words. Quotation marks are used.*
REPORTED SPEECH (c) Ann said (that) *she was* hungry. (d) Tom said (that) *he needed his* pen.	REPORTED SPEECH = giving the idea of a speaker's words. Not all of the exact words are used; pronouns and verb forms may change. Quotation marks are NOT used.* **That** is optional; it is more common in writing than in speaking.

*Quoted speech is also called *direct speech*. Reported speech is also called *indirect speech*.

14-9 Verb Forms in Reported Speech

(a) QUOTED: Joe said, "I *feel* good." (b) REPORTED: Joe said (that) he *felt* good. (c) QUOTED: Ken said, "I *am* happy." (d) REPORTED: Ken said (that) he *was* happy.	In formal English, if the reporting verb (e.g., *said*) is in the past, the verb in the noun clause is often also in a past form, as in (b) and (d).

— Ann said, "I am hungry."
(e) — What did Ann just say? I didn't hear her.
  — She said (that) she *is* hungry.
(f) — What did Ann say when she got home last night?
  — She said (that) she *was* hungry.
	In informal English, often the verb in the noun clause is not changed to a past form, especially when words are reported *soon after* they are said, as in (e).
	
	In *later reporting*, however, or in formal English, a past verb is commonly used, as in (f).

(g) Ann *says* (that) she *is* hungry.	If the reporting verb is present tense (e.g., *says*), no change is made in the noun clause verb.

QUOTED SPEECH	REPORTED SPEECH (formal or later reporting)	REPORTED SPEECH (informal or immediate reporting)
He said, "I *work* hard." He said, "I *am working* hard." He said, "I *worked* hard." He said, "I *have worked* hard." He said, "I *am going to work* hard." He said, "I *will work* hard." He said, "I *can work* hard."	He said he *worked* hard. He said he *was working* hard. He said he *had worked* hard. He said he *had worked* hard. He said he *was going to work* hard. He said he *would work* hard. He said he *could work* hard.	He said he *works* hard. He said he *is working* hard. He said he *worked* hard. He said he *has worked* hard. He said he *is going to work* hard. He said he *will work* hard. He said he *can work* hard.

The security guard said (that) he *had found* an open window.

14-10 Common Reporting Verbs: *Tell, Ask, Answer/Reply*

(a) Kay *said* that* she was hungry. (b) Kay *told me* that she was hungry. (c) Kay *told Tom* that she was hungry. INCORRECT: *Kay told that she was hungry.* INCORRECT: *Kay told to me that she was hungry.* INCORRECT: *Kay said me that she was hungry.*	A main verb that introduces reported speech is called a "reporting verb." **Say** is the most common reporting verb** and is usually followed immediately by a noun clause, as in (a). **Tell** is also commonly used. Note that **told** is followed by **me** in (b) and by **Tom** in (c). **Tell** needs to be followed immediately by a (pro)noun object and then by a noun clause.
(d) QUOTED: Ken asked me, "Are you tired?" REPORTED: Ken *asked (me) if* I was tired. (e) Ken *wanted to know if* I was tired. Ken *wondered if* I was tired. Ken *inquired whether or not* I was tired.	**Asked** is used to report questions. Questions are also reported by using **want to know**, **wonder**, and **inquire**.
(f) QUOTED: I said (to Kay), "I am not tired." REPORTED: I *answered / replied* that I wasn't tired.	The verbs **answer** and **reply** are often used to report replies.

**That is optional. See Chapter 14-8.

Other common reporting verbs: *Kay **announced / **commented** / **complained** / **explained** / **remarked** / **stated** that she was hungry.*

David *asked Elena if* she would marry him.
Elena *said* (that) she wasn't sure.

Appendix
Supplementary Grammar Charts

UNIT A

A-1 The Present Perfect vs. The Past Perfect

Present Perfect	(a) I am not hungry now. I *have* already *eaten*.	The PRESENT PERFECT expresses an activity that *occurred before now, at an unspecified time in the past,* as in (a).
Past Perfect	(b) I was not hungry at 1:00 P.M. I *had* already *eaten*.	The PAST PERFECT expresses an activity that *occurred before **another** time in the past.* In (b): I ate at noon. I was not hungry at 1:00 P.M. because I had already eaten before 1:00 P.M.

I laughed when I saw my son.
He *had poured* a bowl of noodles on top of his head.

A-2 The Past Progressive vs. The Past Perfect

Past Progressive		
	(a) I *was eating* when Bob came.	The PAST PROGRESSIVE expresses an activity that was *in progress at a particular time in the past.* In (a): I began to eat at noon. Bob came at 12:10. My meal was in progress when Bob came.
Past Perfect		
	(b) I *had eaten* when Bob came.	The PAST PERFECT expresses an activity that was *completed before a particular time in the past.* In (b): I finished eating at noon. Bob came at 1:00 P.M. My meal was completed before Bob came.

A-3 Still vs. Anymore

Still	
(a) It was cold yesterday. **It is** *still* **cold** today. **We** *still* **need to** wear coats. (b) The mail didn't come an hour ago. **The mail** *still* **hasn't come.**	***Still*** = A situation continues to exist from past to present without change. ***Still*** is used in either affirmative or negative sentences. Position: midsentence*

Anymore	
(c) I lived in Chicago two years ago, but then I moved to another city. **I don't live in Chicago** *anymore.*	***Anymore*** = A past situation does not continue to exist at present; a past situation has changed. ***Anymore*** has the same meaning as *any longer.* ***Anymore*** is used in negative sentences. Position: end of sentence

*See Chart 1-3, p. 3. A midsentence adverb
  (1) precedes a simple present verb: *We **still need** to wear coats.*
  (2) follows *am, is, are, was, were: It **is still** cold.*
  (3) comes between a helping verb and a main verb: *Bob **has already arrived**.*
  (4) precedes a negative helping verb: *Ann **still hasn't** come.*
  (5) follows the subject in a question: *Have **you already** seen that movie?*

A-4 Additional Verbs Followed by *That*-Clauses*

conclude that	guess that	pretend that	show that
demonstrate that	imagine that	recall that	suspect that
fear that	indicate that	recognize that	teach that
figure out that	observe that	regret that	
find out that	presume that	reveal that	

*See Chart 14-4, p. 98, for more information.

Scientists *have **concluded that*** dolphins can communicate with each other.

A-5 Additional Expressions with *Be* + *That*-Clauses*

be ashamed that	be furious that	be proud that
be amazed that	be horrified that	be terrified that
be astounded that	be impressed that	be thrilled that
be delighted that	be lucky that	
be fortunate that	be positive that	

*See Chart 14-5, p. 99, for more information.

UNIT B: Phrasal Verbs

NOTE: See the *Fundamentals of English Grammar Workbook* appendix for more practice exercises for phrasal verbs.

B-1 Phrasal Verbs

(a) We *put off* our trip. We'll go next month instead of this month. (*put off = postpone*)	In (a): *put off* = a phrasal verb A PHRASAL VERB = a verb and a particle that together have a special meaning. For example, *put off* means "postpone."
(b) Jimmy, *put on* your coat before you go outdoors. (*put on = place clothes on one's body*)	
(c) Someone left the scissors on the table. They didn't belong there. I *put* them *away*. (*put away = put something in its usual or proper place*)	A PARTICLE = a "small word" (e.g., *off, on, away, back*) that is used in a phrasal verb.
(d) After I used the dictionary, I *put* it *back* on the shelf. (*put back = return something to its original place*)	Notice that the phrasal verbs with *put* in (a), (b), (c), and (d) all have different meanings.
Separable	Some phrasal verbs are **separable**: a NOUN OBJECT can either

(e) We *put off our trip*. = (vb + **particle** + NOUN)
(f) We *put our trip off*. = (vb + NOUN + **particle**)
(g) We *put it off*.   = (vb + PRONOUN + **particle**)
	(1) follow the particle, as in (e), OR
	    (2) come between (separate) the verb and the particle, as in (f).
	
	If a phrasal verb is separable, a PRONOUN OBJECT comes between the verb and the particle, as in (g).
	    INCORRECT: We put off it.

Nonseparable	If a phrasal verb is **nonseparable**, a NOUN or PRONOUN always follows (never precedes) the particle, as in (h) and (i).
(h) I *ran into Bob*. = (vb + **particle** + NOUN) (i) I *ran into him*. = (vb + **particle** + PRONOUN)	*INCORRECT: I ran Bob into.* *INCORRECT: I ran him into.*
Phrasal Verbs: Intransitive	Some phrasal verbs are intransitive; i.e., they are not followed by an object.
(j) The machine *broke down*. (k) Please *come in*. (l) I *fell down*.	
Three-Word Phrasal Verbs	Some two-word verbs (e.g., *drop in*) can become three-word verbs (e.g., *drop in on*).
(m) Last night some friends *dropped in*.	In (m): *drop in* is not followed by an object. It is an intransitive phrasal verb (i.e., it is not followed by an object).
(n) Let's *drop in on* Alice this afternoon.	In (n): *drop in on* is a three-word phrasal verb. Three-word phrasal verbs are transitive (they are followed by objects).
(o) We *dropped in on* **her** last week.	In (o): Three-word phrasal verbs are nonseparable (the noun or pronoun follows the phrasal verb).

B-2 Phrasal Verbs: A Reference List

A **ask out** = ask (someone) to go on a date

B **blow out** = extinguish (a match, a candle)
break down = stop functioning properly
break out = happen suddenly
break up = separate, end a relationship
bring back = return
bring up = (1) raise (children)
(2) mention, start to talk about

C **call back** = return a telephone call
call off = cancel
call on = ask (someone) to speak in class
call up = make a telephone call
cheer up = make happier
clean up = make neat and clean
come along (with) = accompany
come from = originate
come in = enter a room or building
come over (to) = visit the speaker's place
cross out = draw a line through
cut out (of) = remove with scissors or knife

D **dress up** = put on nice clothes
drop in (on) = visit without calling first or
without an invitation
drop out (of) = stop attending (school)

E **eat out** = eat outside of one's home

F **fall down** = fall to the ground
figure out = find the solution to a problem
fill in = complete by writing in a blank space
fill out = write information on a form
fill up = fill completely with gas, water, coffee,
etc.
find out (about) = discover information
fool around (with) = have fun while wasting
time

G **get on** = enter a bus/an airplane/a train/a
subway
get out of = leave a car, a taxi

get over = recover from an illness or a shock
get together (with) = join, meet
get through (with) = finish
get up = get out of bed in the morning
give away = donate, get rid of by giving
give back = return (something) to (someone)
give up = quit doing (something) or quit trying
go on = continue
go back (to) = return to a place
go out = not stay home
go over (to) = (1) approach
(2) visit another's home
grow up (in) = become an adult

H **hand in** = give homework, test papers, etc., to
a teacher
hand out = give (something) to this person,
then to that person, then to
another person, etc.
hang around/out (with) = spend time relaxing
hang up = (1) hang on a hanger or a hook
(2) end a telephone conversation
have on = wear
help out = assist (someone)

K **keep away (from)** = not give to
keep on = continue

L **lay off** = stop employment
leave on = (1) not turn off (a light, a machine)
(2) not take off (clothing)
look into = investigate
look over = examine carefully
look out (for) = be careful
look up = look for information in a dictionary,
a telephone directory, an
encyclopedia, etc.

P **pay back** = return borrowed money to
(someone)
pick up = lift
point out = call attention to

(continued)

print out = create a paper copy from a computer

put away = put (something) in its usual or proper place

put back = return (something) to its original place

put down = stop holding or carrying

put off = postpone

put on = put clothes on one's body

put out = extinguish (stop) a fire, a cigarette

R **run into** = meet by chance

run out (of) = finish the supply of (something)

S **set out (for)** = begin a trip

shut off = stop a machine or a light, turn off

sign up (for) = put one's name on a list

show up = come, appear

sit around (with) = sit and do nothing

sit back = put one's back against a chair back

sit down = go from standing to sitting

speak up = speak louder

stand up = go from sitting to standing

start over = begin again

stay up = not go to bed

T **take back** = return

take off = (1) remove clothes from one's body (2) ascend in an airplane

take out = invite out and pay

talk over = discuss

tear down = destroy a building

tear out (of) = remove (paper) by tearing

tear up = tear into small pieces

think over = consider

throw away/out = put in the trash, discard

try on = put on clothing to see if it fits

turn around }
turn back } change to the opposite direction

turn down = decrease the volume

turn off = stop a machine or a light

turn on = start a machine or a light

turn over = turn the top side to the bottom

turn up = increase the volume

W **wake up** = stop sleeping

watch out (for) = be careful

work out = solve

write down = write a note on a piece of paper

Tim wanted the girl next to him to *turn off* her cell phone.

UNIT C: Prepositions

NOTE: See the *Fundamentals of English Grammar Workbook* appendix for practice exercises for preposition combinations.

C-1 Preposition Combinations: Introduction

ADJ + PREP (a) Ali is ***absent from*** class today. V + PREP (b) This book ***belongs to*** me.	*At, from, of, on,* and *to* are examples of prepositions. Prepositions are often combined with adjectives, as in (a), and verbs, as in (b).

C-2 Preposition Combinations: A Reference List

A
be absent from
be accustomed to
   add (*this*) to (*that*)
be acquainted with
   admire (*someone*) for (*something*)
be afraid of
   agree with (*someone*) about (*something*)
be angry at / with (*someone*) about / over (*something*)
   apologize to (*someone*) for (*something*)
   apply for (*something*)
   approve of
   argue with (*someone*) about / over (*something*)
   arrive at (*a building / a room*)
   arrive in (*a city / a country*)
   ask (*someone*) about (*something*)
   ask (*someone*) for (*something*)
be aware of

B
be bad for
   believe in
   belong to
be bored with / by
   borrow (*something*) from (*someone*)

C
be clear to
   combine with
   compare (*this*) to / with (*that*)
   complain to (*someone*) about (*something*)
be composed of
   concentrate on
   consist of
be crazy about
be crowded with
be curious about

D
   depend on (*someone*) for (*something*)
be dependent on (*someone*) for (*something*)

be devoted to
   die of / from
be different from
   disagree with (*someone*) about (*something*)
be disappointed in
   discuss (*something*) with (*someone*)
   divide (*this*) into (*that*)
be divorced from
be done with
   dream about / of
   dream of

E
be engaged to
be equal to
   escape from (*a place*)
be excited about
   excuse (*someone*) for (*something*)
   excuse from
be exhausted from

F
be familiar with
be famous for
   feel about
   feel like
   fill (*something*) with
be finished with
   forgive (*someone*) for (*something*)
be friendly to / with
be frightened of / by
be full of

G
   get rid of
be gone from
be good for
   graduate from

H
happen to
be happy about (*something*)
be happy for (*someone*)
 hear about / of (*something*) from (*someone*)
 help (*someone*) with (*something*)
 hide (*something*) from (*someone*)
 hope for
be hungry for

I
 insist on
be interested in
 introduce (*someone*) to (*someone*)
 invite (*someone*) to (*something*)
be involved in

K
be kind to
 know about

L
 laugh at
 leave for (*a place*)
 listen to
 look at
 look for
 look forward to
 look like

M
be made of
be married to
 matter to
be the matter with
 multiply (*this*) by (*that*)

N
be nervous about
be nice to

O
be opposed to

P
 pay for
be patient with
be pleased with / about
 play with
 point at
be polite to
 prefer (*this*) to (*that*)

be prepared for
 protect (*this*) from (*that*)
be proud of
 provide (*someone*) with

Q
be qualified for

R
 read about
be ready for
be related to
 rely on
be resonsible for

S
be sad about
be satisfied with
be scared of / by
 search for
 separate (*this*) from (*that*)
 be similar to
 speak to / with (*someone*) about (*something*)
 stare at
 subtact (*this*) from (*that*)
be sure of / about

T
 take care of
 talk about (*something*)
 talk to / with (*someone*) about (*something*)
 tell (*someone*) about (*something*)
be terrified of / by
 thank (*someone*) for (*something*)
 think about / of
be thirsty for
be tired from
be tired of
 translate from (*one language*) to (*another*)

U
be used to

W
 wait for
 wait on
 warn about / of
 wonder about
be worried about

Index

A/an, 77–78, 82–83
    (*Look on pages 77 through 78 and also on*
    pages 82 through 83.)
	The numbers following the words listed in the index refer to page numbers in the text.

Consonants, 4*fn.* (*Look at the footnote on page 4.*)	The letters *fn.* mean "footnote." Footnotes are at the bottom of a page or the bottom of a chart.

A

A/an, 77–78, 82–83
A vs. **an**, 77
Accustomed to, 76
Active verbs, 70
Adjective clauses (*a man who lives*), 86–90
Adjectives (*good, beautiful*), defined,
        42, 86
    following *be*, 42, 74
    comparative (*more/-er*) and superlative
        (*most/-est*), 64–65
        with *much, a lot, far*, 66
    following *get* (*get hungry*), 75
    nouns used as (*a flower garden*), 42
    participial (*interesting, interested*), 75
    possessive (*my, our*), 45
Adverb clauses, 62
    with *because*, 62
    with *even though/although*, 62
    if-clauses, 18
Adverbs (*quickly*):
    comparative (*more/-er*) and superlative
        (*most/-est*), 64–66, 68
    frequency (*always, sometimes*), 3
    negative (*seldom, never*), 3
    since-clauses, 21
    time clauses (*before he came*), 13, 18, 21
A few/a little, 80
After, 13, 18, 40
A little/a few, 80

A little (**bit**), 66
A lot, much, far, 66
A lot (**of**), 80
Alike, like, 69
Almost, 63
Already, 23
Although, 62
Always, *etc.* (frequency adverbs), 3
Am, is, are + **-ing** (*am eating*), 1
And, 59–60
    with parallel verbs, 19
    with *so, too, either, neither*, 61
    with subject–verb agreement, 41
Another, 47, 49
Anymore, 23, 104
Answer/reply, 102
Apostrophe (*Tom's*), 44
Articles (*the, a, an*), 82–83
As . . . as comparisons, 63
    not as . . . as vs. *less*, 66
Ask if, 102
As soon as, 13, 18
At, as preposition of time, 40
Auxiliary verbs:
    after *and* and *but*, 19, 60–61
    modal, 50
    in questions, 29
    in short responses to yes/no questions, 28
    in tag questions, 37

B

Be:
in questions, 6
simple past (*was, were*), 7
simple present (*am, is, are*), 1

Be about to, 19

Be + adjective, 42, 74
followed by *that*-clause (*am sorry that*), 99

Because, 62

Before, 13, 18, 27, 40

Be going to, 15–16
vs. *will*, 17

Be + **-ing** (*is/was eating*), 1, 12

Believe so, 99

Be + past participle (*be interested in*), 71, 74
(SEE ALSO Passive)
followed by noun clauses (*be worried that*), 99

Be supposed to, 76

Better:
and *best*, 65
had better, 50, 54
like . . . better, 58

Be used to/accustomed to, 76

But, 60

By:
followed by *-ing* (*by doing*), 93
with passive (*by*-phrase), 70, 73
with reflexive pronoun (*by myself*), 46
vs. *with*, 93

C

Can, 50
ability, 51
permission, 52
polite question, 53

Capitalization, 59, 85

Clauses, defined, 13*fn.*, 86*fn.*, 96*fn.* (SEE ALSO Adjective clauses; Adverb clauses; *If*-clauses; Noun clauses; Time clauses)

Commas:
with adverb clauses, 13, 62
in connecting ideas:
with *and*, 59
with *but* and *or*, 60
vs. periods, 59
in quoted speech, 100

in a series, 60

Comparatives (*more/-er*), 64–66
with adjectives and adverbs, 65
double (*the more . . . the more*), 67
with modifiers, 66
with nouns, 67
repeated (*more and more*), 67

Comparisons, 63–69
as . . . as, 63
comparatives (*more/-er*), 64–65, 68
same, similar, different, like, alike, 69
superlatives (*most/-est*), 64–65, 68

Conjunctions (*and, but, or, so*), 59–60

Consonants, 4*fn.*

Continuous verbs (SEE Progressive verbs)

Contractions of verbs:
with *not:*
hasn't, haven't, 22
isn't, aren't, 1
mustn't, 55
shouldn't, 54
wasn't, weren't, 7
won't, 16
with nouns:
have, has, 24
will, 16
with pronouns:
am, is, are, 1
had, 27, 54
have, has, 22, 24
will, 16
would, 53, 58
with question words, 35
who's vs. *whose,* 32, 90*fn.*
use of, 35

Could, 50
past ability, 51
in polite questions, 53
possibility, present/future, 52

Count/noncount nouns, 78–85
noncount nouns, 78–81

D

Dependent clause, defined, 86*fn.* (SEE ALSO Adjective clauses; Adverb clauses; Noun clauses)

Different from, 69

Direct speech (SEE Quoted speech)

Distance (*to . . . from, how far*), 33

Do as main verb in *what*-questions, 31
Does, do, did:
    in negative (*I don't . . .*), 1, 7
        with *have to*, 55
    in questions (*Did you . . . ?*), 1, 7, 28–29
        with *what*, 31
    in short answers (*Yes, I do*), 6–7, 28
Double comparatives (*the sooner, the*
       better), 67

E

-Ed (*asked, played*), 7, 9
    past participle, 9, 20
        as adjective (*a confused person*), 75
    pronunciation, 11
    spelling, 8
Either, 61
Enough, 95
-Er/more and **-est/most**, 64–66
Even though, 62
Ever, 3, 23
Every, 41
Expressions of quantity (*some, many*), 80, 82

F

Far, much, a lot, 66
Farther/further, 65
(A) few/(a) little, 80
For (purpose) (*I went to the store for*
       milk), 94
For and **since** (time) (*I stayed for two days*),
       21, 23–25
For (*someone*) to do (*something*), with **it**
       (*It is important for you to study*), 94
Frequency:
    adverbs (*always, sometimes*), 3
    expressions (*a lot, every day*), 33
    questions about, with *how often*, 33
From . . . to, to express distance, 33
Full stop (period), 59*fn.*
Future time, 15–19
    be going to and *will*, 15–17
    in *if*-clauses, 18
    immediate (*be about to*), 19
    using present verbs to express (*It begins*
       tomorrow), 18–19
    in time clauses (*Before he comes, we*
       will . . .), 18

G

Gerunds (*riding, working*), 91
    following prepositions, 93
    as subjects (*Riding horses is fun*), 94
    verbs followed by (*enjoy working*), 91–92
Get + adjective/past participle (*get hungry, get*
       tired), 75
Get used to/accustomed to, 76
Go + **-ing** (*go shopping*), 91
Gonna (*going to*), 16

H

Habitual past (*used to do something*), 14
Had:
    contracted with pronouns, 54
    in past perfect (*She had already*
       eaten), 27
Had better (*You'd better study*), 50, 54
Have, auxiliary in present perfect
       (*They have eaten*), 22
    progressive vs. non-action, 5
Have got to, 50, 55
Have to, 50, 55
    do not have to, 55
Helping verbs (SEE Auxiliary verbs; Negatives;
       Questions; individual items)
Hope so, 99
How, 32, 36
    how about, 36
    how come, 30
    how far, 33
    how long, 34
    how many (*times*), 33, 81
    how much, 80–81
    how often, 33

I

If-clauses, 18
    expressing future time in, 18
    as noun clauses, 96, 102
If/whether in noun clauses, 98, 102
Immediate future (*be about to*), 19
Imperative sentences (*Stop!*), 57
In, as preposition of time, 40
Independent clause, defined, 86*fn.*
Indirect speech (SEE Reported speech)

Infinitives (*to eat*), 92
    with *it* (*It is easy to cook eggs*), 94
    with modals (*have to study*), 50
    purpose (*in order to*), 94
    with *too* and *enough*, 95
    verbs followed by, 92
Information questions, 28
***-Ing*:**
    gerund (*Swimming is fun*), 91
    present participle (*They are swimming*), 9
        as adjective (*an interesting book*), 75
        in tenses (SEE Progressive verbs)
    spelling, 8–9
***In order to*,** 94
***Interested* vs. *interesting*,** 75
Intransitive and transitive verbs, 72
Irregular noun plurals (*tomatoes, fish*), 38, 44
Irregular verbs (*eat, ate, eaten*), list, 10
***It*,** to express distance (*It is two miles . . .*), 33
It + infinitive (*It is easy to do*), 94
It + ***take*** (length of time), 34
Its vs. ***it's*,** 45

J

***Just*,** 23
Just (***as . . . as***), 63

L

***The least*,** 68
***Less . . . than*,** 66
***Let's*,** 57
***Like, alike*,** 69
***Like . . . better*,** 58
***Like, love*,** 92*fn.*
***A little/a few*,** 80
Logical conclusion, 56

M

Main clause, 13, 62, 86*fn.*
***Many/much*,** 80
***May*,** 50, 52
    permission, 52–53
    polite question, 53
    possibility, 17, 52

***Maybe*,** 17, 54
    vs. *may be*, 52
Measure, units of (*a cup of, a piece of*), 81
Midsentence adverbs (*usually, seldom*), 3, 23, 104*fn.*
***Might*,** 50, 52
Modal auxiliaries, 50–58 (SEE ALSO individual items)
    in passive, 73
    tag questions with, 56
***More/-er . . . than*,** 64–66
***The most/-est*,** 64–65, 68
***Much, a lot, far*,** 66
***Must*,** 50
    logical conclusion, 56
    necessity, 55
***Must not*,** 55–56

N

***Nearly*,** 63
Negatives:
    adverbs (*seldom, never*), 3
    be + *not*, 1
    be + *not* + *going to*, 16
    past progressive (*was/were not*), 12
    present perfect (*has/have not*), 22
    present progressive (*am/is/are not*), 1
    should + *not* (*shouldn't*), 54
    simple past (*did not*), 7
    simple present (*does/do not*), 1, 6
    will + *not* (*won't*), 16
    (SEE ALSO Contractions of verbs)
***Neither*,** 61
***Never*,** 23
Non-action (nonprogressive) verbs (*know, want, belong*), 5
Noncount nouns (*furniture, mail*), 78–81
    units of measure with (*two cups of tea*), 81
    used as count nouns (*paper* vs. *a paper*), 81
Not (SEE Negatives)
***Not as . . . as*,** 66
Noun clauses, 96–102
    with *if/whether*, 98, 102
    with question words (*what he said*), 97
    reported speech, sequence of tenses, 101
    with *that* (*I think that . . .*), 98–99

Nouns:
    used as adjectives (*a flower garden*), 42
    count/noncount (*chairs/furniture*),
      78–83
    plural forms, 4, 38, 41
    possessive (*Tom's*), 44
    pronunciation of final -*s*, 39
    as subjects and objects, 39

O

Object pronouns, personal (*him, them*), 43
    in adjective clauses (*whom I met*), 88
Objects:
    of a preposition (*on the desk*), 40
    of a verb (*is reading a book*), 39
On, as time preposition (*on Monday*), 40
One of + plural noun, 68
Or, 60
Other, 47–49
Ought to, 50, 54

P

Parallel structure with *and, but, or,* 59–60
    with verbs (*walks and talks, is walking and
      talking*), 19
Particles, in phrasal verbs (*put away*), 106
Participial adjectives (*interested* vs.
    interesting), 75
Partitives (SEE Units of measure)
Passive (*It was mailed by Bob*), 70
    by-phrase, use of, 70, 73
    modal auxiliaries (*should be mailed*), 73
    stative (*is married*), 74
    summary of forms, 71
Past habit (*I used to live in . . .*), 14
Past participles, defined, 9, 20
    as adjectives (*be tired, be surprised*), 74
      following *get* (*get tired*), 75
      vs. -*ing* (*interested* vs. *interesting*), 75
    of irregular verbs, list, 10
    in passive, 70–71
Past perfect (*had left*), 27
    vs. present perfect, 103
Past progressive (*was eating*), 12
    vs. past perfect, 104
Past time, 7–14 (SEE ALSO Tenses)
Period, 59

Personal pronouns (*she, him, they*), 43
Phrasal verbs, list, 107–108
    intransitive, 106
    nonseparable, 106
    separable, 106
    three-word, 106
Phrase, defined, 96*fn.*
Please, 53, 57
Plural nouns, 4, 38 (SEE ALSO Singular
    and plural)
Polite questions using modals (*May I? Would
    you?*), 53, 58
Possessive:
    in adjective clauses (*whose*), 90
    nouns (*Tom's*), 44
    pronouns and adjectives (*mine* and
      my), 45
Prefer, 58
Prepositional phrases (*on the desk*), 40
Prepositions (*at, from, under*):
    combinations with verbs and
      adjectives, 109
    followed by gerunds, 93
    list, 40, 109–110
    objects of, 40
    of place, 41
      vs. time, word order, 41
    used as particle in phrasal verbs (*put off,
      put on*), 106
    placement in adjective clauses, 90
    placement in information questions, 29
    in stative passive (*be married to*), 74
    of time (*in, on, at*), 40
Present participle (*eating*), 9
    as adjective (*interesting*), 75
    vs. gerund, 91
Present perfect (*have eaten*), 20–27
    defined, 24
    vs. past perfect, 103
Present time, 1–6 (SEE ALSO Tenses)
Principal parts of a verb (*eat, ate, eaten,
    eating*), 9
Probably, 17
Progressive verbs (*be* + -*ing*), 9
    vs. non-action (*I am thinking* vs.
      I think), 5
    past (*was doing*), 12
    present (*is doing*), 1, 18, 25
    present perfect (*has been doing*), 25–26

Pronouns:
    in adjective clauses (*who, which*), 87–89
    contractions with (SEE Contractions)
    used as expressions of quantity (*many, some*), 82
    personal (*I, them*), 43
    possessive (*mine, theirs*), 45
    reflexive (*myself, themselves*), 46
Pronunciation:
    -ed, 11
    -s/-es, 39
Punctuation:
    apostrophe (*Tom's*), 44 (SEE ALSO Contractions)
    comma:
        in adverb clauses, 13, 62
        vs. a period, 59
        in quoted speech, 100
        in a series with *and*, 59
    period, 59
    quotation marks, 100
Purpose (*in order to, for*), 94

Q

Quantity, expressions of (*a lot, several*), 80, 82
Question forms, 29
    past progressive (*were you doing?*), 12
    present perfect (*have you done?*), 22
    present perfect progressive (*have they been driving?*), 25
    present progressive (*are you doing?*), 1
    simple past (*did you do?*), 7
    simple present (*do you do?*), 1
    with *will* (*will you do?*), 16
Questions, 28–37
    information (*why, when*), 28, 97
    polite (*would you please?*), 53–54
    possession (*whose car is this?*), 32
    tag (*You know Bob, don't you?*), 37
    yes/no, 6, 28–29
Question words, 29, 35 (SEE ALSO Noun clauses; individual items)
Quite, 63
Quotation marks, 100
Quoted speech, 100

R

Recently, 23
Reflexive pronouns (*myself*), 46

Relative clauses (SEE Adjective clauses)
Reported speech, 100–101

S

-S/-es:
    with plural nouns (*birds*), 4, 38, 78
    pronunciation, 39
    with simple present verbs (*eat*), 1
    spelling, 4
Same, similar, different, like, alike, 69
Say vs. *tell*, 102
-Self/-selves, 46
Sequence of tenses in noun clauses, 101
Several, 80
Shall, 15fn.
Short answers to questions, 6–7, 12, 16, 22, 28
Should, 50, 54
Simple form of a verb, 9
Simple past, 7
    defined, 24
    vs. past progressive, 12
    vs. present perfect, 24
Simple present, 1, 6
    to express future time, 19
    in future time clauses, 18
    vs. present progressive, 2
Since and *for*, 21, 23–25
Singular and plural:
    nouns (*a bird, birds*), 38–39, 78
    nouns used as adjectives (*flower gardens*), 42
    personal pronouns (*I, we*), 43
    possessive nouns (*student's, students'*), 45
    present tense verbs (*eat*), 1, 4
    verbs in adjective clauses (*man who is, men who are*), 89
So:
    with *and* (*and so do I*), 61
    conjunction (*It was late, so we left*), 60
    substituted for *that*-clause (*I think so*), 99
Some, 78, 82
So/too/either/neither, 61
Spelling:
    -ed, 8
    -er/-est, 65
    -ing, 8
    -s/-es, 4, 38

Stative (non-action) verbs, 5*fn.*

Stative passive (*is married*), 74

Still, 23, 104

Subject pronouns, personal (*I, she, they*), 43
    in adjective clauses (*a man who is, a book which was*), 87

Subjects, verbs, objects, 39
    transitive vs. intransitive verbs, 72

Subject–verb agreement, 41
    in adjective clauses, 89

Superlatives, 64–65, 68

Supposed to, 76

S-V-O-P-T, 41

T

Tag questions (*You know Bob, don't you?*), 37
    with modal auxiliaries, 56

Take, with ***it*** to express length of time, 34

Tell vs. ***say, ask***, 102

Tenses:
    past perfect (*had worked*), 27
    past progressive (*were working*), 12
    present perfect (*have worked*), 21–24
    present perfect progressive (*have been working*), 25–26
    present progressive (*is working*), 1
        future meaning, 18
    simple future (*will work*), 15
    simple past (*worked*), 7, 9, 12, 24
    simple present (*works*), 1
        future meaning, 18–19

Than:
    in comparatives (*more/-er*), 64, 66
    following *like better, would rather*, 58

That:
    in adjective clauses (*a book that I read*), 87–90
    in noun clauses (*He said that . . .*), 96, 98–99, 105

The, 82–83
    with names, 84

Their, they're, there, 45

There + be, 41

Think, progressive vs. non-action, 5

Think so, 99

This + morning/afternoon/evening, 15

Three-word verbs, 106 (SEE ALSO Phrasal verbs)

Time clauses, defined, 13
    form, 13
    future, 18
    past, 13
    with *since*, 21

Today, tonight, 15

To . . . from, to express distance, 33

To + simple form (infinitive), 92
    (*in order*) *to*, 94

Too (excess amount), 95
    with *and* (*and I do too*), 61

Transitive and intransitive verbs, 72

Two-word verbs, 106 (SEE ALSO Phrasal verbs)

U

Units of measure (*a cup of, a piece of*), 81

Until, 13, 18

Used to (past habit), 14
    vs. *be used to*, 76

V

Verbs:
    parallel, 19
    principal parts of, 9
    reporting, 101–102
    singular and plural, in adjective clauses, 89
    vs. subjects and objects, 39, 72
    transitive/intransitive, 72
    (SEE ALSO Auxiliary verbs; Modal auxiliaries; Passive; Phrasal verbs; Tenses; individual items)

Very, 66

Vowels, 4*fn.*, 77

W

Was, were, 7, 12
    + *-ing* (*was eating*), 12

What, 30
    in noun clauses, 96–102
    what about, 36
    what . . . for, 30
    what + a form of *do*, 31
    what kind of, 31
    what time vs. *when*, 30

When:
    in noun clauses, 97
    in questions, 29–30
    in time clauses, 12–13, 18
Where, 29–30
    in noun clauses, 96
Whether, 96, 98, 102
Which:
    in adjective clauses, 89
    in noun clauses, 97
    in questions, 31
While, 12–13, 18
Will, 50
    vs. *be going to,* 17
    forms, 16
    future, 15
    in polite questions, 53
    with *probably,* 17
With vs. **by,** 93
Who/who(m):
    in adjective clauses, 87–90
    in noun clauses, 97

    in questions, 29–30
    who's vs. *whose,* 32, 90*fn.*
Whose:
    in adjective clauses, 90
    in noun clauses, 97
    in questions, 32
Why, 30
Why don't, 57
Word order (S-V-O-P-T), 41
Would, 50
    contractions with pronouns, 53, 58
    in polite questions, 53
    in reported speech, 101
Would rather, 58

Y

Yes/no questions, 6, 28–29, 98
Yet, 23

NOTES

NOTES